*This Vast*
  *External Realm*

Books by Dean Acheson

DEAN ACHESON

# This Vast
# External Realm

W · W · NORTON & COMPANY · INC

NEW YORK

Copyright © 1973 by David Acheson

FIRST EDITION

Library of Congress Cataloging in Publication Data
Acheson, Dean Gooderham, 1893–1971.
  This vast external realm.

  1.  United States—Foreign relations—1945–    —
Addresses, essays, lectures.  2.  United States—
Politics and government—1945    —Addresses, essays,
lectures.  I.  Title.
E744.A223  1973      327.73      73–6892
ISBN 0–393–05495–0

1   2   3   4   5   6   7   8   9   0

. . . Not only, as we have shown, is the Federal power over external affairs in origin and essential character different from that over internal affairs, but participation in the exercise of the power is significantly limited. In *this vast external realm,* with its important, complicated, delicate, and manifold problems, the President alone has the power to speak or listen as a representative of the nation. . . .

—Opinion of Mr. Justice Sutherland, for the Court, in *United States* v. *Curtiss-Wright Export Corp.,* 299 U.S. at 319.

# Contents

# Contents

# Foreword

These articles and speeches by Dean Acheson were selected for publication here because (with one exception, dealing with labor relations) they appeared best to express those principles which my father thought cardinal to the successful conduct of foreign affairs. Just as *Present at the Creation* (W. W. Norton, 1969) depicted his experience as Secretary of State, so this book is intended to collect in one place his reflections on the lessons of that experience. The degree to which any of these pieces is or is not topical to today's news or controversies played no part in the selection process. If certain currents of ideas recur from item to item in this collection, it is because they were central to the body of thought that my father distilled from his entire association with "the vast external realm," as the title of this book calls the field of foreign affairs. For this reason, and in this sense, this collection was thought an appropriate supplement to *Present at the Creation.*

11

# Foreword

Much gratitude is owing to Miss Barbara Evans, for many years my father's secretary and collaborator on countless writings, whose orderly documentation and familiarity with many caches of material made the selection process manageable.

*David C. Acheson*
Washington, D.C.
June 1973

# Introduction

Dean Acheson was one of the most distinguished public servants of our times. He was Assistant Secretary, Under Secretary, and finally Secretary of State. After he left the government in 1953, he maintained his interest in foreign affairs. In view of his experience and the depth of his background in foreign affairs, any writings of Dean Acheson must be of interest to those concerned in the foreign relations of this country, and this collection of essays written following his retirement is especially so. All the best qualities of his thinking are brought out here; the clarity of his thought and the lucidity and facility of his expression are present in every one of these essays.

He, like others, considered that our foreign policy was frequently based too much on a simplistic moralism. One can agree with his strictures, but nonetheless recognize, as he says himself in these writings, that the moral element is inevitable and indigenous to the policy of a democracy such as ours.

# Introduction

Dean Acheson gives a brilliant and cogent exposition of many of the fundamentals of a sound foreign policy which are applicable to the dilemmas we face now and are a valuable contribution to our understanding. Above all, they very well illustrate the workings of one of the best minds of our period, and in this respect one's attention will be arrested by the one earlier essay —from the 1930s—on labor relations. Though the remaining essays were written in the latter part of his life, they bring with them the experience and wisdom of many active and valuable years in the direction of American foreign affairs. They show us what we have lost with his passing.

*Charles E. Bohlen*
June 1973

*This Vast*
*External Realm*

# Post-War Foreign Policy: Second Phase

No words of mine can convey to you the depth of my appreciation of your kindness to me this evening. To a sterner nature than mine it may be enough to know that in hard days one did one's best. But it is a lonely satisfaction, and leaves the heart cold. You bring the warmth of a quadruple honor—the Award of the Woodrow Wilson Foundation, bearing the accolade of that great name; the fact that in following my beloved chief, President Truman, in this honor, you associate me with him once again; the presence and the kind words of my colleagues, Mr. Stevenson, Secretary Finletter, and Mr. Lewis, whose friendship now, as always, in Francis Bacon's phrase "redoubleth

Award for Distinguished Service to Dean Acheson, October 1, 1953.

## This Vast External Realm

joys and cutteth griefs in half"; and the attesting presence of this great company of generous friends.

I accept it with a full and grateful heart. The warmth of such friendship makes one stiffening from old wounds feel once again the oar in his hand, the surge of the sea under the stem and the prow pointed to seas never yet sailed. And one feels again the grim courage of that figure at the helm who brought us—not to port, for there will be no port for a long time—but through the hurricane to more navigable seas.

On Labor Day President Truman said that one of the results of private life was that it gave a man time to think. He did not disclose whether the opportunity gave pain or pleasure. I shall not intrude where he has hesitated. But his remark raises another point illustrated by a most able statesman of one of our American neighbors, who was asked his policy about giving public expression to his thoughts. He said: "I have two types of thoughts—one, I share with all; the other I never think."

Your kindness to me tonight gives me an opportunity to share with you some thoughts. Their validity you will judge.

The foreign policy of the United States is composed of two elements, object and method—to put it another way, the purpose or object to be attained, and the various acts, international, domestic, public, and private, which affect our international purposes and goals.

As to the first of these—the broad purpose—I do not believe that, among Americans who are informed, there is or can be any serious disagreement about the proper aim of our foreign policy in the national interest. We would agree, I think, that the purpose of our foreign policy is to maintain and foster an environment in which our national life and individual freedom can survive and prosper. We would believe that the Communist bloc is wholly hostile to the attainment of this purpose; desires a diametrically opposite result; and at one time had, or came close to having, the capacity to effect its desire.

We believe, I continue, that the danger does not confront us alone. It confronts all peoples who wish to pursue their own national or cultural development in their own way, and all who cherish individual liberty. The will and power of some of these nations, added to ours, can obtain the result we and they seek. The support, trust, and cooperation of all is important to us and to them. The loss of certain of these nations would gravely prejudice the outcome.

Such I believe to be the situation in a nutshell. It means, as it had meant five times in the last four hundred years, a coalition to resist the imposition by a powerful state of its hegemony upon others. For it has been by this means that five times a group of states have maintained their independence, their freedom to develop along their chosen paths, however diverse these may have been. A coalition defeated the attempt of Louis XIV to impose absolutism upon Europe, to make subject peoples out of independent peoples. A coalition defeated Napoleon; another defeated the Kaiser; another Hitler. And now another still has been formed to face a danger equal to and greater than any of these—greater because added to the power of a great state is an international conspiratorial doctrine which is used to exacerbate and exploit all conflicts within and between the opposing states.

If, as I believe, this is the problem, let us look at the history of the post-war years. I submit that it falls into two phases: one, the creation of the coalition amid confusion and evident danger; the other, the maintenance and management of the coalition against cajolery and subversion in the face of a more hidden but perhaps greater danger.

The first phase occupied the period from shortly after the end of World War II to the Communist Party Congress in Moscow in the autumn of 1952; the second phase we are now in, and cannot foresee its end, except that it will not come soon.

The problem of the past six years was to create the coalition to oppose the imposition of Communist tyranny. The need to do so came about because the collapse of Germany and Japan removed the powers which stood astride the borders to which five centuries of expansion had brought the Russian Empire. The weakness of Western Europe created a fluidity there, unparalleled in modern times. And the awakening of the peoples of Asia and Africa to a sense of their own destiny released forces both of promise and of confusion.

The task of creating this coalition consisted not merely in bringing the nations concerned together in the common purpose—but almost in recreating the economic and social strength, the moral confidence, and the will to succeed of many, if not most, of the nations involved. It was a task of unprecedented magnitude and difficulty. Nations broken by the war either in spirit, or in substance, or in power, or in all three—friends and former enemies alike—were restored to health and confidence and brought to seek a common purpose.

In this vast and triumphant accomplishment all those nations contributed in effort, in sacrifice, in courage. In furnishing the ways and means—and, I think it fair to say, the inspiration—a major portion of the task fell to the United States.

The steps taken by our own and like-minded nations are too well known to do more than mention them— the prompt action to save Greece and Turkey; the economic restoration, including the Marshall Plan; the lifting of the siege of Berlin; the material and moral rebuilding of Germany and Japan; the North Atlantic Treaty; the creation of the unified military force in Europe and on the Atlantic; the movement for unity in Western Europe, which remains of great importance; the rearmament program; the vindication of collective security in Korea; the Pacific Treaties; and the gallant fight in Indochina, Malaya, the Philippines against Communist-inspired attack.

During this initial post-war period of power fluidity the Russians had successes as well as great and disappointing failures. They tried to win the vital industrial centers of Europe, to complement their system—and failed. Their gain lay in another field—the undeveloped area of China. Their gain here was loss for us. That must be entered in the account.

When this is done and the account of the first phase cast up, one conclusion stands out:

Much, much indeed, has been accomplished in a brief and crowded time. In a very real sense chaos was turned into substance, and substance into strength, by the common will to achieve of free, though deeply tired and tried, peoples. So much so, that last autumn even before the death of Stalin, the Communist Party Congress recognized the profound change, and, in turn, forecast a new Communist policy. No longer did the Party leaders consider constant pressure, the intimidation of vast armaments, ceaseless and violent propaganda, and a hammer-blow or two at weak spots sufficient to accomplish their purpose.

The new Soviet policy was the greatest accolade of our united success. It called for the splitting up of our coalition; the checking and disintegration of our common and growing strength; the end of the United States military participation in the defense of Europe and the Middle East. All this would be accompanied by an expected economic crisis in the West—what Stalin called "the deepening of the general crisis of capitalism." In total, it would create a situation ultimately favorable to Soviet dominance in the world.

And so with our gains and losses, we come to the second phase. Equilibrium has been created. Strength has told. Negotiation is asked, is possible, is desirable, and may—but only may—be productive. This is one of the results we have sought. But negotiation is a method, not an end of policy. In what attitude, with what scale of values, should we approach negotiation? Here certain principles seem to me to contain the essence of salvation.

The first is that never more than at present is the preservation of the coalition so essential. To sustain it and to strengthen it must be the foundation of our foreign policy. The most unforgivable of mistakes would be to falter in a policy just as developments prove its rightness and success.

Let me urge this thought upon you as we approach the coming years. Whatever issues appear upon the conference agenda, whatever debates occupy the columns of the press and the news hours of the radio—the supreme issue, the central point around which all else revolves is the health and strength and cohesiveness of our coalition. Every effort will be made to sow distrust, suspicion, and to make it appear that one or the other of us is imposing upon the others. All of this brings us face to face with the fundamental principles and rules of conduct which govern the association of free peoples in a common effort.

The leadership of a coalition of free peoples requires that the purposes and policies put forward are broad enough to embrace the interests of the whole group—or, at least, the vital essential interests of the group. This is a matter of the deepest moral responsibility. Such a leader is a trustee. His interests cannot be personal or narrow. They must encompass the interests of all for whom he assumes the responsibility of

23

leadership. This conception is essential for the operation of a coalition.

It puts a high price upon leadership. It means that one cannot yield to the demands of domestic politics if the statesmen of the nation exercising leadership are to command the confidence of others, who, in their turn, must subordinate urgent local pressures to the wider good. It means that, in a system of states, the leader, and all others, must deal with the members as one would expect to deal with allies and friends, who have many conflicting points of view. This requires the confinement of issues to the essential and the resistance to pressures which accentuate more remote, divisive issues. A former colleague of mine well said: *"The essence of leadership is the successful resolution of problems and the successful attainment of objectives which impress themselves as being important to those whom one is called upon to lead."*

Leadership also requires courtesy and manners. And at a time when peoples live cheek by jowl with other peoples, it requires not merely diplomatic manners, but governmental, press, radio, and popular manners. Whoever, or whatever seemingly local or personal purpose, insults or denigrates our allies strikes at the heart of our policy. Whoever portrays us as the sole repository of wisdom and resistance to tyranny, and who portrays our allies as something considerably less, does the coalition a great disfavor.

The problems of this fast upsurging phase of our foreign policy are puzzling beyond measure. Those who represent us are entitled to every support. But the point remains that at the heart of our policy always, day in and day out, lies the strengthening of our coalition, of our united front.

And this, in turn, affects touchy points of domestic policy. For without strength—military strength—our own and our allies'—the coalition loses its effectiveness to achieve its essential purpose. If the growth of this strength is stunted or impaired for whatever reason, the same results cannot be expected from our common policy. As a famous critic said of a great actress in the role of Chanticleer, "Charm never made a rooster."

A military force—a unified, collective force—is not made by speeches. A strong economic system of the free world is not made by exhortation and high tariffs. These are some of the costs of responsibility. Our responses to them are tests of maturity. But for historians they will be more—they will bear upon our survival as a nation and a free people.

There is another—and even more difficult—requirement for leadership in our coalition. It is a moral requirement, for the crucial issue of the struggle of our time is a moral issue, one central to the life we have inherited, to the very air we breathe. Above and beyond the alignment of nations and the defensive power which all of us strive to create, inspiring and uniting us, is the idea of freedom—not only national freedom, but the freedom of man. We call our civilization Graeco-Judaic-Christian. The common idea in this heritage is the notion of the dignity of man, which means, as the Age of Enlightenment underlined, the spirit of free inquiry. It is the defense of this idea against the police state, the modern form of tyranny, which unites and inspires the men and women whom our coalition represents and serves.

One of the dangers—clear and present dangers, in judicial phrase—which confronts us Americans is what this struggle may do to us. Do to us, not in the physical or material sense, but in the sense John Milton meant, when he said, "Citizens, it is of no small concern what manner of men ye are, whether to preserve or to lose your liberties." An old French proverb tells us: "Chacun prend à l'adversaire, qu'il le veuille ou non." (Everyone takes on the face of his adversary, whether he wills it or not.)

We are in real danger of taking on the face of our adversary. We see this happening in a number of ways. Each day presents too many examples of callousness, cynicism, indifference to the values of truth, fairness, restraint, free thought, free expression, free inquiry. They occur in many ways and at many levels in our national life.

At the lowest level they appear in the use of totalitarian methods ostensibly to fight Communism. You hear it said, "You have to use the methods of Bolsheviks to beat the Bolsheviks," or "These methods may be rough but so is the enemy." In my view, these rationalizations are insidiously false and deceptive. Bolshevik methods lead to Bolshevism. One of the tragedies of all times is the self-deception of those who act upon the belief that evil means can be justified by, or lead to, good ends.

At a higher and more thoughtful level, but equally

# Post-War Foreign Policy: Second Phase

dangerous, is the view that only by developing an orthodoxy of our own can we defeat the totalitarian orthodoxy. It is said that the Western world wandered from the true path at the time of the Age of Enlightenment, and that the spirit of skepticism and of free inquiry that grew out of that inspired age has so corroded our faith that we are easy prey to the Communists. In my belief, what we need is not less spirit of free inquiry, but more. It has been the central idea of our nation, from the days of 1776 and earlier, that a free society is one in which diversity may flourish, in which the spirit of inquiry and of belief is free to explore and express. The advent of Communism has not changed this. We do not become stronger by imposing a uniformity of thinking upon ourselves; we become weaker. We lose, in fact, what we are fighting for; we take upon ourselves the face of our adversary.

The spirit of free inquiry, free thought, is the kernel of what we are defending, and it is also the strongest weapon in our arsenal. What is more, it is the principal binding force in our coalition. The tradition of 1776 is still the most powerful and attracting force in the world today; it is this that draws to our leadership people all over the world. Without this idea, we are to them just another powerful nation, bent upon interests which are not theirs. If we are narrow, dogmatic, self-centered, afraid, domineering, and crabbed, we shall break apart the alliance on which our future depends. But, if we behave, in our dealings among ourselves and with our allies, as a free society should, we shall succeed in that most difficult task of leading a group of diverse peoples, doing unpleasant and burdensome things, over a long period of time, in the quiet defense of their precious liberty. It may be that this is the highest test of our American civilization which destiny has in store for us.

# "Instant Retaliation":
# The Debate Continued

One might reasonably expect that the normal course of events in 1954 would produce a great national debate on the foreign policy of the United States. This has happened before when an election year coincided with a time of appraisal of far-reaching and costly action by the United States abroad. We had one such debate after the war with Spain and another after the First World War. On these occasions we tried to crawl back into the cocoon of history. For we did not understand that the mold which gave us, from 1814 to 1914, a century of secure withdrawal from the world was broken beyond repair.

From *The New York Times Magazine,* March 28, 1954. The "debate" concerned the policy of "instant retaliation," as stated by Secretary of State Dulles. It had been criticized in an article by Chester Bowles in the *Times Magazine* of February 28.

## This Vast External Realm

The materials from which this protective mold was formed were the balance of power among the great nations of the world and the control of our surrounding seas by a nation well disposed to us and to the world environment in which our free life could exist and flourish. For a hundred years these factors confined the use of force to localized and limited objectives and insured that the sea around us should not be an avenue of attack.

But in 1940 and 1941 we saw, for the second time, our ships destroyed within sight of our coast. Then, enemy blows in the Pacific came dangerously close to opening our western sea approaches. We learned that oceans were no barrier to the new air attack. We learned, too, that no equalization of power was possible if the weight of our own nation was absent from the scales.

Not all at once, but gradually, the facts of the world as it is—contrasted with the world of wishes—hammered at our understanding. Consider for a moment the situation that faced the Western statesmen of 1939. A vast superiority of military strength had been built by three totalitarian powers—Germany, Russia, and Japan. Together, their military might could not be withstood. Separately, only an attack by Japan could predictably be defeated by the Western powers, and this would take—as it did—a major effort. To deal with aggression by either Germany or Russia, the power of the other in the defense was necessary. Moreover, it is now plain that whichever joined in defeating the aggressor would greatly increase its own power. Much of this increase would be achieved by the momentum of military action, some of it in post-hostility operations.

In other words, not only was the balance of power upset in 1939 but even a successful outcome of war would quite certainly leave it upset. And clearly it would remain upset unless the power of the United States continued vigorous and active. But United States military might could not alone prevent an erosion of power on one side and accretion on the other by subversion—working in exhausted societies and aided, when necessary, by the local use of force or threat of force.

So it became increasingly plain as our third post-war debate on foreign policy in half a century went on that the United States was, and must remain, in and of the world, and that coexistence of the victors and the maintenance of peace demanded the recreation of a balancing power to the power of the Soviet system. It demanded a group of nations bound together by the most vital of common interests—their survival as free, independent nations—and willing and able to join in maintaining the integrity and independence of the group; it demanded further that they be ready to help encourage and if necessary protect other nations, even those not intimately associated with them, which had the one essential determination—to maintain their own independence.

This, in turn, meant coalition diplomacy. It meant allies and associates of varying degrees of intimacy, all dedicated to one overriding purpose—to be free and to be no one's satellite.

# This Vast External Realm

In the post-war years the American people discussed these problems many times and agreed with surprising unanimity on the course that our national security demanded.

It would not be surprising, as I said at the outset, if the end of the fighting in Korea brought on a renewal of the discussion. And normally I should have no doubt that this discussion would reaffirm our conviction that the further strengthening of our coalition of free nations is the course of wisdom and safety—in fact, the only right course.

I said "normally" I should have no doubt of this. But there is an abnormal factor present in 1954. To protect our judgment against it we must see it clearly and not underestimate it. This abnormal factor is the use of our current fear of Communism at home to raise doubts about our allies and to attack those, whether Republicans or Democrats, who insist upon the fundamental importance of the coalition policy.

The argument is simplicity itself: France and Italy have substantial Communist parties. Therefore they are unreliable. Britain, India, Pakistan, and others recognize or trade with Communist China. Therefore they are soft on Communists. Do you favor cooperation with these countries? Then you, too, are soft on Communists, unless you favor coercing our allies to change their views.

One thing can be said of this line of argument—it strikes straight at the heart of our policy, past and present. It is the last word in isolationism. It bypasses discussion of the wisdom and necessity of alliances, by seeking to destroy the allies themselves. We must be isolated, because only we are worthy of trust—and not so many of us, at that. It was not by chance that a nation-wide broadcast on Communists in government reached its climax in an attack on Britain.

So those who argue the necessity for increasing the strength and cohesion of the free nations must meet not only the natural tendency to weary of burdens, losses, and responsibilities, but also the sly attack which undermines faith in our allies and among ourselves. It will take more effort and more fortitude than in the past.

Of this I shall not say more, but instead turn to the substance of the discussion. Here the first need is for honest and candid presentation of the facts, of the consequences of various measures, and of the inescapable principles which govern in this field.

For the creation and maintenance of a coalition is governed by principles which are quite immutable and unarguable. They can be disregarded only with the certainty of disaster. They are based upon elemental common sense, with nothing obscure or complicated about them.

A first principle must be clear to everyone. The purpose of action in coalition policy must be to strengthen the coalition and bind it more closely together—or to weaken an opposing coalition and loosen its bonds. If it does either, the action is successful. If it does both, it is very successful. If, on the other hand, the action weakens or divides our own coalition, it is harmful. If it does both, it is very harmful.

# This Vast External Realm

This rule must be an ever-present guide and measure of policy. There are no exceptions. Every violation of it, as of a law of nature, exacts its payment. There comes a point when violations destroy the coalition. Moreover, in applying the rule we must be brutally and mercilessly honest with ourselves in ascertaining the facts and in stating exactly what we are proposing to do. Here the slick statement, the wishful analysis, and the ambiguous, pious generality deceive only ourselves. They do not change the effect of the action for good or ill.

One more basic principle is necessary for our present purposes. A coalition is held together either predominantly by force employed by the leader, or predominantly by the consent of the members. If it is held together predominantly by force, the element of coercion will tend to increase. If it is held together by consent, the members must believe that the bulk of their basic interests are recognized by the leader and served by the coalition. They must believe that the dangers and risks of not being a member of the coalition are greater than the dangers and risks of being a member. If they do not so believe, consent will not be given.

Our post-war development of a series of intersecting coalitions was based upon a clear understanding and application of these principles. It was a vigorous and sustained initiative in a field of action where our moral and physical resources gave us a great advantage. Only the grossest perversion of fact and history can describe the Rio Treaty, the Greek-Turkish program, the Marshall Plan, NATO, the military assistance program, and the German, Japanese, Philippine, and Anzus treaties as other than powerfully creative. They brought into being new strength and new alignments.

But there is an initiative which the United States and her allies cannot seize—the initiative in aggression. The policy of a democracy or of a group of democracies cannot include aggression. It would violate the deepest moral convictions of the people who are the final arbiters of policy, and of their profound attachment to peace and justice under law. Our very institutions preclude it, for aggression must be conceived in secret and executed by stealth. We must by our very nature be defenders, not offenders.

That is the basis of our moral position in the world. And to make it appear that we have the initiative in this field through our so-called massive retaliatory power is a fraud upon the words and upon the facts. Retaliation is not initiative, but is the reaction to someone else's initiative. So by all means let us abide by the cardinal principle of being scrupulously honest with ourselves.

A sound policy for a coalition of free nations held together by their freely given consent must have an offensive and a defensive side. These are not alternative; they are complementary. They must go forward simultaneously—as, indeed, they have in the past.

The offensive program was designed to, and did, increase the strength and unity of the coalition and the strength and independence of nations, free but not associated with it. It was designed to further the interests of all the participating nations.

The defensive program was intended to, and did, counter the use of force against members of the coalition and nations, not members, who were determined to remain free.

Such a program must be designed to protect the interests of all the nations concerned. It cannot be successful if it sacrifices the interests of some nations to others. It will certainly fail as a coalition policy if it sacrifices the interests of all the other nations to those of one.

Two types of aggression must be provided against: (1) a strike at a vital point which shows a willingness by the aggressor to perpetrate or accept World War III; (2) an attack which may be disguised as civil war and which must be resisted, but not by methods that make probable the mutual destruction of a general war.

Until 1950 the insidious and dangerous possibilities in the second form of aggression were not fully understood. It was thought, or perhaps hoped, that the danger of alienating world opinion in the "cold war" and the risk of invoking our striking power with atomic weapons in a "hot" war would deter any use of armed force in aggression. But Korea showed that this was not so. There the attack had to be met—and was met—on the ground where it occurred. And this, in turn, required the raising, equipping, supplying, and

# "Instant Retaliation": The Debate Continued

training of forces, our own and others, which could do this.

So a sound military program which will encompass the interests of all the nations associated with us requires an atomic striking force with power so great that the mutual suicide of general war will be rejected by all. It requires also forces that can deal on the spot with lesser aggressions which, if unchecked, would go far to undermine the integrity, and certainly the power, of the free world.

If it is said, as it sometimes has been, that we cannot afford another war like Korea, the answer is that such a war is the only kind that we or anyone else can afford. Only a madman would attempt to avoid it by plunging into the unspeakable disaster of a world war.

Now the military program we have been discussing cannot be acquired on the cheap. It is very expensive indeed. The cost of retaliatory striking power effective to deter general war requires more than we are now spending. For as a deterrent not only is it necessary that we should be able to punish the enemy, but also it is necessary that we should minimize to the full extent possible his ability to punish us and our allies. For the equation has two sides—what the enemy gains versus what he suffers. If he stands to gain less than he suffers, the deterrent is all the greater. And this means defensive as well as striking power—an air defense of which we have far too little and a civilian defense of which we have none. Here the costs are great.

But, assuming that we have or obtain retaliatory

striking power and the complementary air and civilian defense system effective to deter general war, have our needs and the needs of our coalition been met? It may be suggested that they have, and that the threat to use this power at places of our own choosing will deter lesser aggressions.

Let us examine the consequences of this idea in more detail. The plan of meeting any aggression with massive retaliation in places of our own choosing certainly suggests that we propose to strike not at the place that the aggressor group has chosen but at some other place. Presumably this is a place more vital to them, a place which would hurt them badly. It would be foolish to assume that this would not produce counter-retaliation, which would hurt us as much, or perhaps more, and would be designed to prevent any further strikes by us. And then we would be in World War III.

So the threat means that we would meet any aggression by precipitating World War III. Clearly we would not and could not mean this. Anyone with any knowledge of our country and our people would know this.

Strategic atomic bombing is not our first but our last resort, reserved for the dread occasion when we must meet an all-out attack with the full attendant horrors of atomic war. No responsible, certainly no democratic, government would use it on any lesser occasion. Indeed the very suggestion that it be so used implies the prior end of democratic government as we know it, because of the very necessity for secrecy in decision and execution. So, as a threat, which we do not mean, the policy would not deter.

And what if it did not deter? What would happen if we were called and the chips were down? The gravest consequences would be likely to follow. Our own coalition would be divided and weakened.

Divided, because our allies would rightly believe that their very existence was being recklessly exposed to unnecessary risks; their consent to such a coalition policy could not be expected; their consent to the use by us of bases in their territory could likewise not be expected.

Weakened, because the joint will and strength of the group to hold together and resist encroachments would be diminished, if not separated into ineffective parts, without adequate forces to meet the aggression where it occurred.

But this is not all. The cohesion of the aggressor group would be increased by the necessity of even greater reliance on the Soviet Union as the only possessor of atomic power to counterbalance ours. Furthermore, other nations not associated with either coalition but anxious to maintain their independence would be alienated from us by what they would undoubtedly regard as an immoral and reckless program calculated to plunge them into general turmoil and misery.

In short, it would be difficult to violate more completely the principles upon which successful coalition policy must be founded.

# This Vast External Realm

The alternative is to rely upon the defensive power of ourselves and our allies and upon our own defensive atomic striking power to deter all concerned from the overwhelming disaster of general war; and, in addition, to provide the means—adapted to the needs of, and consistent with, coalition policy—to meet piecemeal or creeping aggression.

This is expensive, very expensive, in human, financial, and physical resources. It means that we and our allies must be prepared to commit men to battle in far-off places and that our men and people should willingly accept this burdensome task, if the need arises. If we are not willing to do this, we shall not carry, or be entitled to carry, much weight.

We shall be told that such a program will bankrupt us. If what is meant by this is that the American economy is not capable of supporting what is necessary for its own survival, I do not believe it.

Our people are living better than they or any people in the world have ever lived. Our agricultural surpluses are a grave embarrassment. Our steel industry, the greatest in the world, is running at only 75 per cent of capacity. Our average consumer expenditures are five times greater than those of the average Russian consumer. Our own and our allies' productive capacity and resources greatly exceed those of the group which makes these problems for us.

Our difficulty is not one of means. The means exist and will be put to use when leadership evokes the will to do so. Our people have not in the past failed in will and determination when their leaders have frankly and honestly laid the facts and necessities before them.

Unfortunately, it is easier to present easy and comfortable courses than hard and difficult ones. Tax cuts and reduced expenditures are more popular than the task of providing, in men, money, and materials, a military program adequate to meet the dangers before us. Munich, with its promise of peace in our time, was popular—until a year later war swept away the illusions it created.

This democracy and the coalition it leads are lost if the competition for leadership becomes a competition in promising cheap and mechanical solutions to dangers which can only be met by effort long sustained, by clear and cool heads, and by the coverage which made and preserved this country.

# Meetings at the Summit:
# A Study in Diplomatic Method

There are fashions in everything, even in horrors, as the appearance of the chemise dress makes us so acutely aware. By the couturier's alchemy our most curvaceous charmers are turned into bags of Idaho's famous product. So, as Mr. Louis Halle points out in a book published in April, *Choice for Survival* (Harper & Brothers), there are fashions in alarms, fashions which change, not because the dangers which inspired them have diminished, but because they seem to us less likely to occur, and because, also, our attention has been distracted by a new alarm.

After the First World War, Mr. Halle reminds us, attention was concentrated—and rightly so—on the horror of chemical warfare. It was pointed out that whole

Lecture given by Dean Acheson as part of the Distinguished Lecture Series·of the University of New Hampshire, May 8, 1958.

cities and even larger areas could be wiped out in a few minutes by known gases. Today even more lethal ones, and far better means of delivering them, are known. The danger is greater, not less, than it was thirty or forty years ago. The same is true of bacteriological warfare, which could destroy us even more effectively and on a larger scale.

But fears of these dangers, writes Mr. Halle, have "apparently been forgotten by us . . . now that nuclear weapons have become the fashionable and fascinating preoccupation" of the Russians, ourselves, and most literate people. The preoccupation is all-pervasive. The danger is real enough, in all conscience. With the development of the intercontinental and intermediate-range ballistic missile, it has come to seem catastrophically imminent.

As a result, the urgent demand for relief from constant anxiety over nuclear destruction presses on all governments subject to popular control, and can be skillfully stimulated by those that are not. Curiously enough, it does not seem to occur to us that the same missiles which make so menacing the danger of atomic destruction could, alternatively, carry almost equally dangerous chemical or bacteriological weapons, though these weapons might not have the same potential to destroy the power to retaliate.

But, be that as it may, the demand for relief is urgent; and just as there are fashions in fears, there are fashions in remedies. The present cure for all impending hazards is the conference at the summit. A large part of its appeal—like that of all slogans—is the association of ideas which Mr. Churchill's unfortunately catchy phrase arouses. "The summit" summons up all man's aspirations—"A banner with a strange device, Excelsior!" The summit is where God dwells, from which Lucifer was cast out, and, as lightning, fell to the outermost depths. "Nations," said Bagehot, "touch at their summits"—but the summit he spoke of was the social summit found in the drawing rooms of the aristocracy. "An Ambassador," he wrote, "is not simply an agent; he is also a spectacle. . . . An aristocracy is in its nature better suited to such work; it is trained to the theatrical part of life; it is fit for that if it is fit for anything."

Bagehot is perhaps out of date as a recruiting officer for the Foreign Service, but his conception of diplomatic method, conducted privately, in high, but not necessarily the highest, circles, and with style, is worthy of thought.

Between the summit of popular conception where walk the gods who, so legend goes, can bring order out of the tangled affairs of men, and the depths of our anxiety and despair, there seems to lie only the workaday world, where men like ourselves—perhaps with a little more knowledge, but no more wisdom—created the sorry mess in the first place. So, on to the summit! —hoping that those who go will be transmuted on the way into gods; and forgetting the Arab proverb that the ass which went to Mecca remained an ass.

Apparently, whatever the outlook and the consequences, to the summit we are going. A French writer puts it this way: ". . . objections and conditions put forward in the first place have disappeared as if by magic. It has been enough for the Soviets to send letter after letter and message after message, signed Bulganin, to have their way." And he does not like the prospect at all.

> The Western democracies are suffering a new diplomatic defeat. . . . And they are courting a more serious one still, since the conference called by Moscow can only serve the interests of the Soviet Empire.
>
> In fact, the "conference at the summit" cannot change any essential element of the conflict between the U.S.S.R. and the U.S.A. . . . In going to it the non-Communist participants will put themselves in the dilemma of subscribing to the presentations of Khrushchev and Company or as appearing responsible for a fiasco, and so, as "war-mongers" or zealots for "positions of strength" in the language of the Communist propaganda.

At this point we might ask ourselves where this idea of meetings at the summit, as distinct from the phrase, came from, what we know about their history, and whether, under present conditions, they hold much hope of solving the world's problems.

The first of these high gatherings in modern times was brought together in the seventeenth century, after six years of negotiation, to end, if possible, the Thirty Years' War. It consisted of two assemblies: the representatives of the Catholic states of France and the Holy Roman Empire meeting at Münster; those of Sweden and the Protestant estates of the Empire, at Osnabrück. In neither assembly was there present a chief of state. The two assemblies were a single congress. Their discussions went on for more than four years. So did the war. Two treaties, called collectively the Treaty of Westphalia, came out of these talks, both signed on October 24, 1648. They provided for numerous transfers of territory, a payment of indemnity to Sweden, confirmation of the three religious communities within the Empire, some toleration for minority religious groups, and, finally, far-reaching constitutional changes in the structure of the Empire. They represented the desire of an exhausted Europe, devastated, with a considerable part of its population killed, to end fighting which it no longer had the capacity or will to continue.

Those in the Western democracies who urge a meeting at the summit do not, as I read them, look for so sweeping a settlement. But what of the Russians? The French writer I quoted a moment ago ventures this estimate of Russian purpose: "Stalin's successors intend to have their conquests growing out of the last war, what they call the territorial *status quo*, recognized, and to pursue the domination of the planet under cover of non-aggression pacts containing the inevitable clause for non-interference in the internal affairs of the parties. The 'conference at the summit' has no other purpose."

This, of course, does not contemplate a settlement of the war, but a continuance of it by other means— and the meeting at the summit is one, and an important one, of those means. But let us return to the record of these high meetings.

The greatest one after Westphalia was the Congress

of Vienna. Here again Europe, exhausted and disrupted after more than a decade of total war, having finally defeated France and sent Napoleon to Elba, disposed of his empire and established a political settlement which endured for half a century, and greatly influenced another half century. The final treaty was signed after eight months of negotiation on June 9, 1815, and was ratified nine days later by the Battle of Waterloo.

The Congress of Vienna was only partially a meeting at the summit. Alexander I of Russia was the Russian government and attended in person. Metternich and von Hardenberg were the principal ministers of the Austrian and Prussian monarchs and acted for them. The ablest and most effective men present were Lord Castlereagh, Foreign Minister and leader of the House of Commons, and the Prince de Talleyrand, Foreign Minister of the restored Bourbon monarch, Louis XVIII. The Congress sat for eight months.

The Congress of Berlin, in 1878, operated on a different principle. It put into treaty form, and obtained agreement to, understandings reached by most of the participants before the meeting. But this task took a month to accomplish. The purpose was to bring about a Balkan settlement, where crisis had been precipitated by Turkish misrule, Russian invasion and occupation of the outskirts of Constantinople, British naval support of Turkey, and Austrian ambitions in Bosnia and Herzegovina. No settlement could endure long in that troubled and unstable area; but this one lasted for nearly thirty years.

Two nations were represented at the conference by

giants, very close to the summit—Germany by Prince von Bismarck, who assumed the rule of "honest broker"—though the Russians later disputed the adjective; and Great Britain by Benjamin Disraeli, Lord Beaconsfield, "der alte jude," as Bismarck called him with reluctant respect. The other participants were of lesser stature and rank.

We may pass the Algeciras Conference, held in 1906 to compromise French-German rivalries in Morocco. It was neither a summit conference nor of enduring importance. But it marked the beginning of American interest in international conferences; for President Theodore Roosevelt, because of his close relations with the French and German ambassadors in Washington, played an important part and influenced its deliberations.

With this introduction, the curtain rises on the great international conferences of our own day, at the summit and below it. They begin, of course, with the Conference of Paris, which sat for the first six months of 1919 to produce a settlement after the First World War. Here nothing was worked out in advance, though much was, erroneously, thought to have been. The eminence of the participants was equalled only by the extent of their failure. For the first time an American President, Woodrow Wilson, represented the United States. Speaking for Great Britain were the Prime Minister, Lloyd George, and the Foreign Minister, A. J. Balfour; for France, the great Clemenceau; for Italy, the Prime Minister, Orlando. Thirty and more other countries were represented by prime ministers, foreign ministers, or emirs. Such famous names as Paderewski, Venizelos, and Smuts appeared in the roster. A vast bureaucracy, which for a time included Maynard Keynes, was in attendance.

Perhaps the failure was inevitable. Russia was in revolution; Eastern Europe in turmoil. The European allies were more persuaded that in one form or another the war against Germany should be carried on (the blockade of Germany continued until July 7, 1919) than that an enduring settlement was possible. Furthermore, the treaties with Austria, Bulgaria, Hungary, and Turkey, also laid out in Paris, dissolved authority in Eastern Europe, the Balkans, and the Middle East, without making possible the viability of the new states or stable conditions within or between them.

President Wilson stubbornly adhered to theoretical notions and moralistic precepts even while his actions were oriented by masters in the art of maneuver. None of the Big Four perceived the true nature of their problems or the consequences of their actions, or the strength of the forces which they were attempting to control, or their own weakness. Or, perhaps one should say that, if they perceived the nature and direction of their problems, they did not bend their wills to the solution of these problems.

As soon as the terms of the treaty were known, General von Seeckt began the policy of collaboration with the Russian general staff in the manufacture of arms and the training of German (and Russian) forces in Russia, which circumvented the disarmament and neutralization of Germany. It was von Seeckt's Reichswehr which formed the nucleus of Hitler's formidable armies. Thus the power of Russia and Germany began to recover and grow while that of the European allies was developing the virus which would bring it to collapse. A good part of the apparent settlement reached at Paris and embodied in the five treaties—Versailles, Saint Germain, Trianon, Neuilly, and Sèvres—had begun to disintegrate within a decade, and what remained was swept away by Hitler in the next decade.

The years between the World Wars brought us several international conferences. The first, the Washington Conference of 1921, was a disaster; the others, failures.

The Washington Conference was called to consider limitation of armaments and Pacific and Far Eastern questions. It took three months to do this. Nine powers, which did not include Germany or Russia, were represented by delegations of eminent men—the United States, by Secretary of State Hughes, Mr. Elihu Root, and Senators Lodge and Underwood; Great Britain, by, among others, Mr. Balfour, then Lord President of the Council, and Sir Robert Borden, who had recently retired as Prime Minister of Canada; France, by M. Briand, who was both Prime Minister and Foreign Minister, and M. Viviani, then in private life. The pattern of the other delegations was similar.

In the field of armaments the French blocked any action regarding armies. They also blocked the British effort to "ban," as we would say nowadays, the submarine. But the conference, nothing daunted, subjected the submarine to a rule of law drafted by Mr. Root. Submarines were subject to the international law of visit and search and forbidden to destroy commerce. This became, perhaps, their principal use by all parties in the Second World War.

But the grave error came in the distribution of power in the Western Pacific which the conference effected. In order to terminate the Anglo-Japanese alliance, about which this country had become obsessed, and to get agreement on some principles regarding China, Mr. Hughes scrapped the great naval building program upon which the country had embarked. He also agreed not to fortify Guam, the Philippines, and the Aleutians. The Japanese, on the other hand, behind the device of an iron curtain proceeded to fortify the mandated islands—for which we paid so heavily in the Second World War. These arrangements and the 5–3 naval ratio established with Japan made it impossible for us to deploy effective naval strength in the Far East *and* the Atlantic simultaneously, and abandoned the Western Pacific and Eastern Asia to Japan.

In a decade the Japanese had moved into Manchuria and then, through Shanghai, into North China, despite their undertakings in the Nine Power Treaty to respect the sovereignty, the independence, and the territorial and administrative integrity of China. In another decade Japanese dominion extended throughout East and Southeast Asia, all the way to the Bay of Bengal; and the United States Pacific battleship fleet lay at the bottom of Pearl Harbor. All in all, we cannot afford many conferences like the Washington Conference of 1921.

In extenuation two pleas may be made. One is that, even without the treaty, we would not have created the naval strength necessary to have maintained peace and stability in the Western Pacific. Under Presidents Coolidge and Hoover the navy was not built up to the limits permitted by the treaty. The other is that the treaties were thoroughly in accord with the spirit of the times. They were immensely popular. Ratified by the Senate with only one dissenting vote, they were hailed by the *New York Tribune* as "a monumental contribution to international understanding and human progress," and by the *Baltimore Sun* as a "stupendous success—the results epochal." Mr. Lippmann thought that Mr. Hughes had "stopped the drift into a ruinous and indecisive war." He was wrong about this. The war came just twenty years later; while it may perhaps be described as "ruinous," it can hardly be called "indecisive." These considerations explain, but do not vindicate, American policy in the conference.

The Genoa Conference of 1922 retains still an unmistakably comic aspect. All the parties involved were pursuing purposes different from those they avowed. In the end, the outcasts of European society, the Russians, through the wily Chicherin outsmarted them all. Genoa was the shortest conference we have mentioned. It lasted just over five weeks and then, like an old soldier, just faded away.

# Meetings at the Summit

The Soviet Union, mistaking the purpose of Genoa, eagerly accepted its first invitation into polite society. The Russians believed that it offered an ideal field for the maneuver and propaganda envisaged by Chicherin's proposal "to consider the claims of the powers against Russia and of Russia against the powers, and to draw up a definite treaty of peace between them." They discovered too late that under Lloyd George's oily description of the purpose of the conference, as "a united effort . . . to remedy the paralysis of the European system," lay a Franco-British scheme to confront Russia with a European consortium with which all Russian external trade must be conducted. This would have turned the tables on Chicherin's plan to confront foreign capitalist enterprises with the monolith of Russian state trading. But Chicherin had a secret weapon which, if adroitly used, could blow the solid front of the consortium wide open; and Chicherin was nothing if not adroit.

For some time the "Easterners" in the German foreign office had been at work with the Russians in their mutual desire to supplement Soviet-German military arrangements with an economic treaty. The treaty was to provide for cross-forgiveness of reparations (a horrid thought to the West), assumption of diplomatic and consular relations, preferential treatment in trade and economic matters, and a provision (aimed at the consortium) that neither country would enter into an international arrangement for dealing with the other's economic requirements without a "previous exchange of opinions with the other."

The Russians wanted to sign the treaty before Genoa, but Rathenau, the German Foreign Minister, knew that this would destroy the conference, and, with it, the hope which he believed it offered for improvement of Germany's position. So he went to the conference technically uncommitted. For a week Lloyd George studiously ignored him and refused to meet with him. Instead the British Prime Minister showered attention on Chicherin. Rathenau became more and more depressed. The Russians, he believed, were being seduced by the British. The Russians encouraged this belief. The German Chancellor, Wirth, urged an attempt to sign with the Russians before it was too late. Rathenau hesitated, waiting for the British invitation which never came.

Finally, on the Saturday night before Easter, about midnight, the Russians, who had in reality made little progress, telephoned from the village of Rapallo, got the Germans out of bed, and before Easter dawned had signed the Treaty of Rapallo.

The result was the explosion of a bombshell. The known economic articles of the treaty were staggering enough. But was there a secret military pact? "The existence of one is believed in," said General von Seeckt, and added, "Is it to our interest to destroy this far-fetched illusion?"

That Easter was not a happy one for the Western statesmen at Genoa. Lloyd George made a gallant effort to resuscitate the conference by suggesting a general pact of non-aggression; but this meeting at the summit was moving rapidly to its fade-out. That was accomplished by a method to be used again over thirty years later. Its agenda was turned over to a mixed group of experts—who faded away, too.

Not long afterward, in the autumn of 1925, another modern conference characteristic cropped up at Locarno. The high contemporary reputation of that conference came more from the favorable propaganda which was put out about it than from any intrinsic accomplishments. At the time it was said to have opened a new chapter in history. In 1925 the "spirit of Locarno" was an inspiring a phrase as was, thirty years later for a shorter time, "the spirit of Geneva." Locarno, it was said, marked the end of the war period and the beginning of an era of peace full of hope and promise. Between the European parties the sovereign right to make war was abolished, mutual security guarantees were given, supported by commitments that all would join the defence of a victim of aggression. Germany agreed to submit to arbitration disputes with her neighbors to the east and west, and was to apply for membership in the League of Nations. Locarno was to be the dawn of a new day, and to mark it Austen Chamberlain was made a Knight of the Most Noble Order of the Garter.

Beneath the propaganda and before the conference there had been long and careful preparation. Each of the statesmen involved wanted a new day, but a different day. Stresemann, who had become Foreign Minister on Rathenau's assassination, wanted the evacuation of the Ruhr and, as a mark of Germany's restored status, her admission to the League of Nations, but without

55

commitment to join in sanctions against Russia; Chamberlain wanted a limitation of Britain's security commitments in Eastern Europe; Briand wanted at least the appearance of a united European front against Russia.

Stresemann went to Locarno armed with a new trade treaty with the Soviet Union. This helped toward reassuring Chicherin that Locarno was not the beginning of a Western orientation of German foreign policy. It was also a good bargaining weapon with the Western allies because of the threat it implied of a further political step. This step Stresemann had refused to take before the conference, but did take in the treaty of Berlin, a few months after it, when obstacles at Geneva to Germany's entry into the League had to be blown out of the way.

The conference sat for only two weeks, but it may fairly be said that it had been in preparation for three years and by many men. Not the least of the preparatory steps was the Dawes Plan of 1924, which, by solving the reparations problem, made possible the evacuation of the Ruhr. But the reputation of the conference was, alas, as ephemeral as its achievements. Both went down like ninepins before Hitler's march into the Rhineland in 1936. That set the course which led on to the Second World War, and with it to the great wartime conferences—Cairo, Teheran, Yalta, and Potsdam.

These wartime conferences, while very much at the summit, were not conferences of the type which we have been considering and about which there is so much talk today. Although, as we shall see, they had some political and diplomatic aspects, these were ancillary to their principal purpose. For, in essence, they were military staff meetings at the highest levels. Their function was to determine, so far as men had choice, the strategy of military operations; allocate priorities between theaters of war; plan the campaigns within them; allocate resources of men, materials, and productive plant among fighting forces on land, sea, and in the air; allocate transport and supplies and equipment of every sort for the military forces and civilian populations.

In such meetings, I suspect that the question of the ends which could, in reality, be achieved by the war seemed almost entirely determined by the state of war itself. Take the decision made at Casablanca to demand "unconditional surrender." It seemed to strengthen the allies against the idea of a separate peace by any of them; and it brought to our own people a sense of historical unity with General U. S. Grant in his reply to General Buckner commanding at Fort Donelson. Those who made it did not, perhaps, perceive that the stable peace we sought would depend less on the mechanisms of an international organization than on a balance of power, which a war policy of unconditional surrender would help to destroy. But even so, to make such balance of power possible, while bringing the war to a desirable end, would have presented the greatest difficulty. For the German government was quite as intractable during the war as the Soviet government was after its end. Moreover, communication with the

Germans was even more difficult, and they were waging war with great competence and vigor on a wide scale.

So the preoccupation of these conferences was chiefly with military strategy. Their story has been told admirably in three books: briefly, and from the American point of view, in Professor Samuel E. Morison's *Strategy and Compromise* (Atlantic, Little, Brown, 1958); at greater length and with fascinating sidelights and opinions from Lord Alanbrooke's war diaries in Sir Arthur Bryant's *The Turn of the Tide* (Doubleday, 1957); and with completeness and objectivity in Dr. Herbert Feis's *Churchill, Roosevelt, Stalin* (Princeton University Press, 1957).

These conferences were essential, and their military decisions as right as it is given to fallible men to be in these matters. Russian suspicions that the Western allies were not doing all they could were resolvable only by staff talks. Furthermore, between the British and American soldiers differing ideas of strategy could be compromised and settled only by bringing the chiefs of staff together in the presence of the supreme authority on each side—President Roosevelt, the Commander-in-Chief, and Mr. Churchill, Prime Minister and Minister of Defense. Agreement through compromise came to the divided chiefs of staff through—to use a later phrase of Mr. Churchill's—"mutual terror." Any compromise by themselves was preferable to what might be done at the summit, if the stalemate continued lower down.

The political deliberations of these meetings did not

have such satisfactory results. I have said that they were ancillary to strategic necessities. Some, for instance, were in the nature of concessions to obtain agreement, as the declaration that Formosa and the Pescadores were to be returned to China was to compensate for disappointing the Generalissimo's expectations of military supplies and activity in the China, Burma, India theater; or as the concession of the Kuriles and rights in Manchuria to the Russians was in aid of the reasonably supposed desirability of obtaining Russian intervention in the war against Japan. Other decisions were to deal with matters which could not be put off, such as what to do with surrendered Italy, or how to prevent a clash between Anglo-American and Russian troops when they should meet in Germany. Some lines of demarcation were essential. Drawing them had to combine prophecy (as to where the troops would be) and the desires of the parties (as to where they wanted them to be).

Still other agreements at Yalta, dealing with Eastern Europe, were made in the hope, destined to be disappointed, of putting some restraint on the unlimited power of Russian arms to establish whatever governments—and, indeed, states—Stalin chose in Eastern Europe. Still another, the adoption at Quebec of the Morgenthau proposal for a pastoral Germany, seemed to have no immediate necessity or ultimate utility.

Of the last of these meetings, Mr. Truman has written: "The most urgent reason for going to Potsdam . . . was to get from Stalin a personal reaffirmation of Russia's entry into the war against Japan, a matter which our military chiefs were most anxious to clinch. This I was able to get from Stalin in the very first days of the conference." This, an agreement on military operations, is all that is worth remembering about Potsdam. With one exception none of its agreements outlived the next three years. All the rest—arrangements for four-power control of Germany and Berlin, dismantling of German industry, reparations, and so on—all became casualties of the cold war.

The exception was the creation of the Council of Foreign Ministers, composed of those of the Soviet Union, the United States, the United Kingdom, and France. China was to be entitled to participation on Far Eastern matters, but, in practice, always encountered a blackball. The outrage committed by this institution upon diplomatic method is equalled only by its cruelty to already oppressed men—the Western foreign ministers. It has rendered their offices unfit for human habitation. That of the Soviet Foreign Minister was already a sure road to obloquy, as Messrs. Litvinov, Molotov, and Shepilov can bear witness. One of my former colleagues used to say that, except for Molotov before and during the last war, the Soviet Foreign Minister was a lesser official engaged in dealing insincerely with the capitalist powers.

To the Council of Foreign Ministers were referred all the questions which the Potsdam Conference could not decide, as well as insoluble ones which arose later, together with the preparation of peace treaties. Up to January 21, 1953, unhappy Secretaries of State attended 218 sessions of this Council, which is no council at all. To this must be added the innumerable other meetings of international bodies. Secretary Byrnes tells that of his 562 days' tenure in the State Department, 350 were spent at international meetings.

All this would be a small price if it brought the world nearer to a stable, or even an unstable, peace. But it has not done so. The Council of Foreign Ministers has been only a rather ineffective method of political warfare. Ineffective, because the Communist areas are pretty well insulated from Western reach, because a destroyer can be more reckless and dramatic than a builder, and because the best political warfare lies in the field of action. The vast fortunes spent on propaganda and advertising are evidence that the repetition of words must have its effect. But words are uttered against a background. A background of such action as the Greek-Turkish policy of 1947 or the Marshall Plan gives the accompanying words the force of truth and relevance. A background of inaction and lethargy brands them with their shamelessness.

The futility and boredom of these meetings, amounting almost to physical pain, with their long unresponsive speeches, each one made in three languages and addressed not to those around the table but to the briefing officers who would twice a day leak them to the press—this is obviously endurable. The evil of them is the distraction of so large a proportion of the top command of the Western foreign offices from positive action. The Council of Foreign Ministers is not an instrument for international communication. It has become a corruption and degradation of a process of communication—by the same methods with which Communists have corrupted and degraded all procedures and institutions designed to bring restraint, order, and manners into human relationships. I marvel at my own magnanimity when, recalling that I know the American diplomat who invented this instrument of torture, I find that I still like him.

While these meetings of the Council of Foreign Ministers were not meetings at the summit, their personnel was, on the average, as close to the summit as attended conferences until Paris, or perhaps Berlin. Certainly, with the exception of Alexander I at Vienna, no chief of state participated in these meetings until President Wilson created the precedent at Paris. His latest successor to emulate him was President Eisenhower at Geneva in 1955. A look at this experience will serve to pull together some conclusions from this excursion into diplomatic history.

The stage revealed as the curtain rose on Geneva seemed the ideal background for the dawn of a new era. Stalin was dead; Beria, executed; and Malenkov, dismissed. Bulganin and Khrushchev, with Marshal Zhukov, President Eisenhower's comrade-in-arms, controlling the army, appeared to be veering towards a relaxation of the cold war, a breathing spell in the East-West struggle. The collapses of France in Indochina and the sulky withdrawal of the United States from the resulting settlement gave the Communists the satisfying sense that they could get more than they gave in settling disputed fields. They seized the opportunity to improve their international position by liquidating the liability of the occupation of Austria. The French destruction of the European Defense Community, and the uncertainty of the future of NATO under the patched-up substitute plan, led to an increased desire in Europe to seek some solution in a meeting at the summit.

The Geneva Conference met without pre-agreed agenda and lasted for six days. During those six days and for very few months afterward the achievement of the conference was believed colossal. Hopes of a new era had been fulfilled. The participants said so, and correspondents spread the glad tidings by written and spoken word.

President Eisenhower with charm and vivacity proposed discussion of the unification of Germany by free elections, liberation of the satellites, a security arrangement for Europe, the exchange of "a complete blueprint of our military establishment," open skies for aerial inspection, and restoration of communication and trade. Unhappy Mr. Eden—so soon to crash, deserted by his American friend, with his career and health in ruins—still believed that the treaty of Locarno was a good model and proposed to base a new security treaty upon it. M. Faure of France made his lesser contribution.

Here, indeed, was the menu of a feast for the gods at the summit. The Russians approached the table with gusto. They talked long and earnestly, and, as the others had done, proclaimed their unalterable devotion to peace. They gave dinners, they proposed toasts; they were photographed in the full ferocity of their friendliness. Amid all this, it quite escaped attention that they refused any discussion of the satellites, proposed the inclusion of Communist China, dismissed German unification, and made disarmament proposals wholly opposed to those suggested by the West.

The conference ended in a blaze of optimism. President Eisenhower had, it was said, completely erased the impression of American belligerency so studiously cultivated by his Secretary of State. As for the untouched agenda, I hardly need say what happened to that. It was, of course, referred to the Foreign Ministers.

Dutifully they met in Geneva from October 27 to November 16, 1955. One who has not been through such meetings might be puzzled as to why it took so long for the Russians to reject every single proposal which had been made to them at the summit; but, in the end, they did. It is reported that in private conversation at Geneva President Eisenhower spoke deprecatingly to the Russians about reports of arms sales to Egypt, and that the Russians expressed the belief that this must relate to some transaction of another country but that they would take care of it. They did. They sent Shepilov to Egypt to sign up. Here ended the "spirit of Geneva."

Geneva was not merely a failure; it was a fraud and positive harm. It brought relaxation to the West just when the need was for endurance. "Heroism, the Caucasian mountaineers say, is endurance for one moment more." So wrote Mr. George Kennan, the distinguished uncle of the present distinguished bearer of that name. Geneva made that "one moment more" impossible.

As we contemplate this story of past international congresses and conferences, does not the mere narrative suggest some conclusions? Does it not suggest, for instance, that unless the situation which brings the conference together is ripe for settlement, then, no matter how eminent the participants, how perceptive their insight, how bold and imaginative their conceptions, their efforts will fail?

The Thirty Years' War cried out for settlement; even the driving force of bigotry was spent; sheer exhaustion provided that degree of moderation which made it possible to offer concessions and to accept far less than was desired or might, perhaps, be won. The case was nearly the same at Vienna, though one must enter a caveat. If Waterloo had been won by Napoleon—and it might well have been—no such settlement would have been possible so long as he controlled the power of France.

On the other hand, the tragedy of the Paris Conference flowed from two sources. The state of affairs with which it had to deal came close to precluding a settlement. Then, also, the "Big Four" aggravated the world's ulcers. The vast turmoil of Russia in revolution, of Germany defeated but not conquered, of Eastern Europe, the Balkans, and the Middle East without established authority, of France and Britain grievously wounded without knowing the extent—all this recalls to me the remark of a friend, now dead, Sir Willmott

Lewis, Washington correspondent of the *London Times*. "We have chaos," he said then, "but not enough to make a world." Then, too, there was no Creator at Paris to make one.

I am inclined to believe that this is true today. Because the catastrophe of nuclear war cannot be exaggerated, nuclear disarmament does not thereby become possible. Armaments cannot be dealt with apart from the character and depth of the political differences between the parties and the possibility of an accommodation between them.

Differences are too great for accommodation where the situation is very volatile and unstable, where at any time the winner may take all. Stability is increasingly gained, as I have urged elsewhere, as Europe becomes stronger, more capable of self-reliance, more united, more able to solve European problems. It is aided, too, as weapons development becomes more predictable and measurable.

These are preconditions for any successful outcome of negotiations with Russians. They are by no means impossible conditions. To achieve them however, requires the re-establishment of confidence and understanding between Western Europe and the United States. It requires long and sympathetic negotiations between these allies, some measure of agreement on values, priorities, and measures, some considerable degree of common and successful action.

The world situation is too fluid to permit of settlement. Let us go back for a moment to our French commentator and recall his estimate of Russian purposes in wishing a summit conference. These were, he wrote, "to have their conquests growing out of the last war, what they call the territorial *status quo,* recognized, and to pursue the domination of the planet under cover of non-aggression pacts." This estimate of Russian purposes seems to me correct; but I also think it true that, at present the territorial *status quo* is not an acceptable basis of a settlement either to the U.S.S.R. or to the United States. This is so because to each the position of the other seems to be deteriorating, to have in it the elements of its own disintegration. Therefore, for either to accept the position of the other would be to accept something which the other had not securely attained—indeed, might be in the process of losing.

For either to attempt by direct action to disturb the *status quo* is far too dangerous, particularly when the value, which it would seek to gain, would seem likely to be achieved in measurable time without incurring this risk. Furthermore, the conference at the summit is an instrumentality by which the Russians plainly believe they can speed the disintegration of the Western position without incurring risk. It offers the unique opportunity to carry on the cold war in the name of peace and by the processes usually associated with the search for peace. By this method, our French commentator pointed out, the United States can be faced with the dilemma of according some degree of recognition to Soviet conquests or of appearing responsible for a fiasco by war-mongering, or—to use the latest cliché—by "inflexibility."

## This Vast External Realm

This suggests to us the second conclusion from our historical survey—that in the last twelve years the international conference has ceased to be an instrument for ending conflict and has become one for continuing it. This has happened not only because the Communists have expertly adapted it to that purpose. The use of negotiation as a method of warfare antedates the Soviet state. A classic example was the negotiation conducted at Canton by the Chinese with Lord Napier of Merchiston, representative of the British Crown, in the 1830's, as brilliantly recounted in *Foreign Mud* by Maurice Collis (Alfred A. Knopf, 1947). But the use of negotiation by the Communists at Brest-Litovsk in 1917–18 and Panmunjom in 1951–1953 was worthy of the model.

The corruption of the conference has occurred, also, because modern media of communication and the development of propaganda have destroyed its usefulness as an instrument for reaching adjustment. The ending of the blockade of Berlin could never have been brought about by an international conference. Indeed, the intervention of the United Nations was utterly fruitless. The settlement was brought about by signals from Moscow which was recognized but not proclaimed, and were then followed up by conversations in corridors by persons who appeared to have no authority or connection with the matter at all. It was only after secret negotiations and understandings that public changes of position became possible.

In short, the international conference has been so used for political warfare, that it is not likely to be useful now except for registering, and getting peripheral consent to, adjustments reached elsewhere, when adjustment is possible.

The third conclusion grows out of the two preceding ones. For high international negotiation, whether or not in conferences, it is not necessary that chiefs of state or heads of governments be involved. Indeed, it is better that they should not be. The makers of ultimate decisions must be insulated a little from the negotiators themselves. They must remain more detached. Neither their prestige nor their judgment should be caught up by the ebb and flow of the struggle in the negotiating chamber. Any commander-in-chief would be unwise to put himself in a forward command post in personal charge of the first assault columns. In particular, this is unwise when the metaphor gains added force by reason of the almost exclusive use of conferences for political warfare. It becomes triply unwise when, as in the United States, the offices of chief of state and head of government are combined.

In the United States the power of the presidential office is equalled only by its vulnerability. Its legal and extra-legal powers, when wisely and courageously used, are almost irresistible forces with which to unify and lead the nation. But, if the President allows himself to become personally involved in negotiation, the possibility of being outmaneuvered and unwisely committed is great. Secretary Dulles has said that after all a summit meeting is the President's meeting. And that is just what it is. Pride and stubbornness may combine to deflect cool and detached judgment, and he may lay himself open to destruction by the Congress. Mr. Wilson found this out after Paris. But Mr. Frank I. Cobb before the event saw the dangers of his personal involvement. On November 4, 1918, he gave Colonel House a memorandum, which was passed on to the President, in which Mr. Cobb wrote:

> The moment President Wilson sits at the council table with these Prime Ministers and Foreign Secretaries he has lost all the power that comes from distance and detachment. . . . he becomes merely a negotiator dealing with other negotiators. He is . . . bound to abide by the will of the majority or disrupt its proceedings. . . . Any public protest to which the President gave utterance would thus be only the complaint of a thwarted and disappointed negotiator. . . .
>
> In Washington President Wilson has the ear of the whole world. . . . If his representatives are balked by the representatives of the other Powers, . . . he can go before Congress and appeal to the conscience and hope of mankind. . . . This is a mighty weapon, but if the President were to participate personally in the proceedings, it would be a broken stick.

President Wilson followed his own contrary judgment to his destruction. Cardinal Wolsey's words are sadly applicable. "And when he falls, he falls like Lucifer, never to hope again." Into the abyss with him went the interests and the prestige of the United States.

If this was true, and indeed it was of Mr. Wilson, it is a thousand times more true today when international conferences are plainly instruments of political warfare. Mr. Khrushchev is insulated from his own people, and can hardly lose, whatever way the battle goes. The heads of our allied governments are likely to leave unpleasant firmness—in today's lexicon "rigidity"—to the American President, and gain what domestic kudos they can from an "imaginative" or "flexible" attitude.

The result of this is to put well nigh irresistible pressure on the President's staff to perpetrate a fraud, to "come up with" some spuriously clever trick or maneuver which will give the illusion of that most valued of all things in America today, "a new idea," which enables one to "grasp the initiative" and give, for a brief moment, the illusion of success—as at Geneva. No constitutional practice would be more undesirable than for the President to be involved in this sort of performance. His participation in international conferences should stop now before it becomes obligatory. No less an authority than President Eisenhower, in his press conference of April 16th, last, indicated agreement with these views. The practice today rests on only two precedents—Paris and Geneva—which should be regarded as examples of what to avoid. The military staff talks of the war years are not, as I have said, precedents here.

What then should be done? We can, I think, adapt our diplomatic method to the present situation more wisely and with more regard to the conservation of our resources than we are now doing. It is probable that from time to time conferences of some sort will take place. They are obviously an important instrument of warfare in the Russian arsenal. Partly because of war-time memories, and partly from despondency induced by the anemic condition of American diplomacy, our allies can be so tempted by Russian overtures and pressed by their publics that we may well lose more in the end by not agreeing than by agreeing to a meeting. It is wise, however, first of all, to expose thoroughly and patiently the nature of the operation which is about to take place.

Then, as I have said, the President should not be involved. Neither should the Secretary of State. The longer these meetings last, the clearer their nature becomes; and a Secretary who is really doing his job cannot do it during the weeks and weeks which these meetings consume. Mr. Byrnes and General Marshall could give instructive testimony here. The President should have another representative for this purpose.

One immediately thinks of the Vice President, but this would be wrong. We are looking, not for an office, but for a man, and it is useful to think of the desirable qualifications. First the negative ones. He should not be an ambitious politician on the make. The tempta-tion of publicity and the appearance of personal suc-cess would be too great for him. He should not believe that he "knows how to get along with the Russians" or that it is his personal task to produce a settlement. On the positive side, he should be forceful in counseling his government and in representing it. He should be a man of character to inspire confidence, and a disci-plined man.

This is not, as some may suppose, the description of

an ideal not to be found in human form. There are men active today who meet the specifications. If, to avoid controversy we look to an older generation, they would clearly have been met by Colonel Henry L. Stimson or General George C. Marshall. The man we seek need not perform this arduous duty more than once; unless he should wish to; and if the title of Personal Representative of the President, or Chief of Delegation, or Ambassador-at-Large needs to be upgraded, why not give him the personal title and rank of Foreign Minister?

But more fundamental than this is the necessity of our recognizing that negotiation today, whether at conferences or elsewhere, must be conducted against the background of all that we do and all that is going on in the world. Action is the most important part of negotiation. It provides the atmosphere and determines the strengths and weaknesses of the participants. The Russians understand very well the great advantage to them of a post-Sputnik conference over, say, the one called in 1947 in Paris to consider the offer of the Marshall Plan. From this they withdrew in considerable disarray, dragging the reluctant Czechs behind them. The idea of a successful foreign policy for the United States, or negotiation by the United States, apart from action, is wholly unreal. For us a recumbent government and a dynamic foreign policy are contradictions in terms. We must do our best within our power—which is great, if we use it wisely— to affect and shape events, not merely tread our way artfully between and around them.

## This Vast External Realm

Once we thoroughly understand this and are prepared to act with continuity and perseverance, we can, I am wholly convinced, create an environment in which Soviet ambitions inconsistent with the basic interests of others will wither to the point where adjustment, the true purpose of honest negotiation, can take place. This delicate process is not likely to occur in the glare and blare of a conference at the summit.

# On Dealing with Russia: An Inside View

Out of Prime Minister Macmillan's March discussions with President Eisenhower have come some rather confused reports. Mr. James Reston, of this estimable newspaper, has said that they are the consequences of an information "policy of faith, Hope and Hagerty, and of these the greatest is faith." At any rate, Mr. Peter Hope, the British Foreign Office's spokesman, described President Eisenhower's commitment to attend a summit meeting in the summer as "unconditional" and without regard to the outcome of a preliminary Foreign Ministers conference.

This was confusing because the President had said, in his earlier broadcast to the nation, that the results

From *The New York Times Magazine*, April 12, 1959.

of this meeting would determine whether it would be worth while for the heads of government to meet later on. Mr. Hagerty, not usually a reticent man, did not qualify Mr. Hope's somewhat startling revelation.

To be sure, the American note sent to the Kremlin says that "as soon as developments in the Foreign Ministers meeting justify holding a summit conference," the Western Governments will participate. But Mr. Hope had already indicated that "justify" was used in its—to employ a word of art—"flexible" sense. As so used, it is not likely to cause Mr. Gromyko's mask to become more mobile, or his capacity to speak without revealing thought to be reduced appreciably, or his hand to be tipped.

There is a good deal of folklore about on the subject of negotiating with the Russians. At the moment, the British, with the authority of those who have just been there, are giving currency to some of its more dubious maxims.

It may be wise to pause and examine some of the observations being put out. All in all, they cover a pretty broad field. We are told, for instance, that since only Mr. Khrushchev can make decisions for the Russian Government, meetings at lower levels are foredoomed to failure; therefore, on to the summit. Again, that "the tragic experience of Geneva in 1955" came from "a grandstand conference," and that this summer's meeting should be held in private. Another suggestion is to hold a series of summit conferences at which the heads of government take up one matter after another, decide them, and let the lower echelons work out the details.

So far as substance is concerned, Mr. Drew Middleton of *The Times* has expressed the British view in somewhat euphemistic terms. The British would seek, he says, stronger guarantees for Berlin in exchange for a "move gradually to meet the Soviet desire for a stabilization of the situation in Eastern Europe." One of the steps in this move, so *The London Observer* reports, is to be a "freezing of East and West forces, or a ceiling on them, in a zone extending either side of the Iron Curtain and beyond Germany."

Is it true that the only way to work anything out with the Soviet Government is by conference with the top man and his staff?

The answer is that it depends on what one is trying to work out. Matters as complex as the concerting of military and supply operations on a vast scale during a world war did require this method. Yet the method, as method, contributed nothing to real agreement on the solution of Eastern European questions. On the other hand, in 1949, arrangements for the ending of the blockade of Berlin were agreed to without meetings at any level. It depends on what the Russians find it in their interests to do.

Let us have a closer look at the events of 1949. After the coup in Czechoslovakia, Stalin had decided, in Khrushchev's later phrase, to cut out the "cancer" of Berlin. So, following the reform of West German currency, a serious problem for East Germany, the blockade of Berlin began in 1948. The United States responded with the airlift (which probably would not work today) and by a counter-blockade of East Germany. The Russians became the losers both in Germany and in their general propaganda position.

Then, at the end of January, 1949, the Soviet Government published answers by Stalin to questions submitted by a newspaper correspondent. One of these questions and its answer were most interesting. The question was whether the Soviet Government would raise the blockade if the Western powers agreed to postpone the formation of a West German state pending a meeting of Foreign Ministers to consider the problem of Germany as a whole. The answer given to this is worth quoting in full:

"Provided the United States of America, Great Britain and France observe the conditions set forth in the third question, the Soviet Government sees no obstacles to lifting the transport restrictions on the understanding, however, that transport and trade restrictions introduced by the three powers should be lifted simultaneously."

Officers in the State Department believed that this might be a signal that the Soviet Government was ready to discuss an end to the blockade and counter-blockade. It was decided that the Secretary of State, in a press conference, should give a signal back.

This took the form of a bland discussion of the questions and answers in the Stalin interview. No great importance was attributed to them. It was pointed out that the formation of a West German Government could hardly be a cause of the blockade since it had not been thought of when the blockade was imposed and was not imminent at the time. Certainly the measures taken in response to the blockade would end when it did. Finally, there were these two paragraphs:

> There are many ways in which a serious proposal by the Soviet Government to restore normal interzonal communications and communications with and within Berlin could be made. All channels are open for any suggestions to that end. The United States, together with the other Western occupying powers, would, of course, consider carefully any proposal made to solve the Berlin problem consistent with their rights, their duties, their obligations as occupying powers.
>
> As I say, all of the normal channels are open. I hope you will not take it amiss if I point out that if I on my part were seeking to give assurance of seriousness of purpose, I would choose some other channel than the channel of a press interview.

At the same time, a senior diplomatic officer attending a United Nations meeting was instructed to say quite casually to a senior Russian officer at the same meeting that he had been interested in the answers recently in the press and wondered whether they suggested anything more than the strict words of the text. The Russian officer had no information; but if he learned anything he would pass it on. In a week he did, equally casually. The answer had been carefully prepared in Moscow. If the American officer had any specific question the Russian would do his best to get an answer.

# This Vast External Realm

Thus began a protracted and highly secret negotiation. The very fact that secrecy was preserved was to each of the parties a sign of the good faith of the other. In the end, it was agreed that the blockade measures on both sides would be ended, a Foreign Ministers' meeting convened on the German problem, and no obligation incurred to postpone action on a West German Government since there was plenty of time for the meeting to be held before, in the normal course of events, any further steps would be taken. As the negotiations finished, other parties were brought in; they approved the plan and joined in the announcement.

The conference of Foreign Ministers which followed two weeks and accomplished almost nothing. It was an exercise in propaganda over Germany. The Russians had exhausted their capacity for adjustment, and further progress must await the development of new realities.

Now, let us bring all this into focus on today's problems. If the Russians believe, which I do not think they do, that their interests would be served by liquidating their offensive against Berlin, they are capable of doing this without a conference at the summit or elsewhere. They might demand, as a price, a conference of some sort to put the limelight of propaganda on what they might think was a new soft spot. But this would follow their decision and not be its cause.

Today, however, they do not wish to end their offensive against Berlin; they want to push it to success. The conference which they seek is designed not to be a cover for their yielding but for the yielding of the West.

# On Dealing with Russia: An Inside View

This brings us to the second of the illusions we have mentioned about negotiating with the Russians. This is contained within the belief that it is possible to have "private" and not "grandstand" conferences of heads of governments.

President Eisenhower does not share this illusion. "It is rather difficult," he said recently, "to visualize such a thing. If you meet with a group of world leaders, it is rather hard to keep the spotlight off of it." And how does one talk informally with "batteries of interpreters and recorders and all that sort of thing? It would almost inevitably change, I think, into something rather formal."

The illusion, however, goes deeper than the belief that it is *possible* to keep these meetings private and out of the spotlight. It goes to a misconception of the role of these meetings in the Russians' strategy or negotiation. The purpose of these meetings to them is not, through discussion of a subject, to reach a resolution of it or an accommodation regarding it. These meetings are acts in themselves which are intended to affect the relative positions of the parties.

The Soviets negotiate by acts and not by debate, offer and counter-offer. Their purpose may be to separate allies, or to undermine governments with their people, or to win over uncommitted peoples. Or it may be, as in "the tragic experience of Geneva in 1955," to bring a sense of relaxation, goodwill, and security, before some energetic offensive such as Soviet intervention in the Middle East.

Publicity is the lifeblood of such an operation. It is

81

not merely, as President Eisenhower thinks, that a meeting of world leaders attracts the spotlight. It is that the purposes of the Russian leaders demand the spotlight, for the spotlight makes an act out of a speech.

Here, too, the Soviet leaders have built-in advantage, for the spotlight shines brilliantly throughout the Free World and stops at the Iron Curtain which rings their own. Their opponents and all who may support or sympathize with them are open and eager to be worked upon. But the Communist people are immune from any counter-offensive, and hear only what their rulers wish them to hear. The dice are loaded in this game.

The conclusion is not, of course, that the Western powers must not go to these conferences. But it is an illusion to expect much from them, or to identify them with the process of negotiation, in the usual sense of the word. They should be recognized for what they are: dangerous and highly mobile adversary operations, in which a cumbersome four-party control, matched against the finger-tip variety, will do pretty well to score a tie.

The most elementary precautions require that the four pilots have a pretty concerted view of the hazards of the operation, the objective of their opponent, and both the strategy and tactics they may jointly have to follow. As things are, one is not so sure that some bad collisions are not inevitable. Take, particularly, the idea of a "move gradually to meet the Soviet desire for a stabilization of the situation in Eastern Europe" and a "freezing of East and West forces . . . in a zone

extending either side of the Iron Curtain and beyond Germany."

This combination of words would not win a prize
for clarity. But, if one might hazard an interpretation,
they seem to mean that the West would accept indefi-
nite Soviet domination of Eastern Europe and insure it
by agreeing to the *status quo* of military power from
Eastern Poland to—and, perhaps, including—France.

This *status quo* would give preponderant power to
the Soviet bloc. Doubtless there are some who would
defend such a policy as a realistic evaluation of, and
adjustment to, the ratio of power in Europe. They,
would do well to pause and think back.

Just twenty-two years ago another British Prime
Minister made a careful, well thought-out, not un-
intelligent appraisal of these factors and acted upon it
quite coolly and deliberately. Let us turn to Mr. Sebastian Haffner's description of the 1937 situation in
*The London Observer* of September 28, 1958:

> Now Germany had, without meeting serious oppo-
> sition, rearmed again and was making territorial de-
> mands backed by real power. Dealing with these de-
> mands was no longer a question of "calling Hitler's
> bluff." The question to be faced was whether to resist
> Germany at the very real risk of another war or whether
> to accept the new balance of power and adjust European
> frontiers and alliances accordingly, in favor of Germany
> and an agreement with her.
>
> Mr. Chamberlain, the new British Prime Minister,
> faced this question squarely and took his decision in
> favor of the second alternative. . . .
>
> This scheme amounted, in effect, to the renegotiation,

among the four great powers, of a new European peace settlement without a preceding renewal of war. The new settlement was to be based on the existing true balance of power, which meant a revision of the 1919 treaties in favor of Germany and, to a lesser extent, of Italy. Germany and Italy were to be made, by territorial concessions and extensions of their spheres of influence, contented and saturated powers like France and Britain; the new territorial settlement was to be underwritten and guaranteed by all four powers; and it was then to be capped by the establishment of a new four-power concert of Europe, permanent mutual consultation, re-entry of Germany and Italy into the League of Nations, and disarmament.

If this scheme—which incidentally, was the last essay in world leadership on the part of Britain—succeeded, it meant peace for at least a generation, and also, for the same time, the preservation of Europe's global preponderance and the postponement of the world revolution which the Second World War was to unleash.

The essence of the scheme was "to anticipate public German demands by private offers and to take and maintain the initiative." And this is where it failed. In the first place, Hitler did not want to be *given* what he demanded; he wanted to *take* it. In the second place, his demands came too fast to be satisfied by orderly processes of negotiation. The pace became more and more breathless until Hitler tired of the farce and moved against Poland.

The proposals mentioned above strike one as substantially similar to Mr. Chamberlain's scheme, but the parallel is not wholly complete. Khrushchev has no prejudice against being given what he wants. He is also willing to move in a more dignified way in receiving what Hitler before him had wanted—the domination of Europe—just so long as the West does not dilly-dally about it. He knows, or believes he does, the direction in which power ratios are moving, and wants European relations to the Soviet Union and the United States adjusted accordingly.

One of the morals of this is that, while dealings with the Soviet Union are in some respects unique, in their fundamentals they are not. Another moral is that, in dealing with the Soviet Union, the prime requisite is to be honest with ourselves. "Negotiation" and "flexibility" are very fine words, but if we really mean "retreat," if we mean "a move gradually to meet the Soviet desire for the stabilization of the situation in Eastern Europe" and a freeze of forces in Central Europe, it would be much better to be frank with ourselves.

For then we would all know that what we are proposing to do is to neutralize Western Germany, and to make impossible any defensive force in Western Europe except the threat of nuclear retaliation from America. With the growth of Russian nuclear power to a position of practical equality this threat loses its credibility.

But the chief moral of all is that we should realize the facts and act upon them. One such fact is that, whether we like it or not, we are on a moving belt which is going to the summit. The question is no longer whether to go, but when, and what to do when we get there.

Another such fact is that at this conference what transpires—the proposals and counter-proposals, the moves and counter-moves—will be, like the shadows on the wall of Plato's cave, reflections from the real world outside. If, as is the fact, we are failing to keep pace, as we could, with the rapid developments in the field of nuclear power, and have actually discarded all the increase in our conventional power created during the Korean crisis, our shadow on the conference table becomes pallid and emaciated.

If, with determined energy, we reverse these catastrophic tendencies; if, in addition, we increase our strength in Europe as—so we are told—the Supreme Commander has urged, then our shadow becomes more solid, because the strength of our position has become so. We can and should be ready, as we have been on occasions in the past, to use ingenuity in devising ways to give the Soviet Union reasonable assurance of its own security and demonstrate our willingness to remove causes of anxiety, if any there really are. The negotiations at Geneva over the past years have had this purpose.

But one thing we should never do. That is to undermine the security of Western Europe—and with it the best hope we have for avoiding resort to nuclear war —by destroying the possibility of developing such a strong defensive position on the ground in Europe that any aggressor contemplating a move against it must contemplate an attack on so large a scale that nuclear war would almost certainly result. Only such a situation makes strategic nuclear power a credible threat and an effective deterrent.

It is because the Russian purpose in disturbing the *status quo* in Berlin seems, as already pointed out, clearly directed to making any military strength in Europe impossible that one can hardly hope for much more from the conference than a return to the negotiations interrupted by the move against Berlin, and an end to that move. But one not given to pessimism may with reason fear that the Russian purpose and some of the proposals of our ally discussed here could bring disaster.

# Fifty Years After

      The autumn, fifty years ago, was an important time for *The Yale Review* and for the author of this article. Both made their debut in New Haven. The author was older than the *Review* by eighteen years; but both—the *Review* vicariously, through its editors and contributors—were children of the nineteenth century, which lived on through the opening years of the twentieth to the early, warm days of August 1914. Looking back now, that time seems wholly unreal, like a traveler's tale of strange and exotic places and people. Not only was it the time of our national youth, but a special sort of youth. Youth without hope can be bitter and tragic, as many have learned in the intervening years, but this continent in 1911 was living in the days of man's innocency.

    The world was stable and predictable. During the

From *The Yale Review,* Vol. LI, No. 1 (October 1961).

hundred years after Waterloo Englishmen and Americans believed themselves moving on the great current of Progress to the reign of universal peace and universal law. So this country's principal effort in the field of foreign policy at the turn of the century was to negotiate arbitration treaties, few of which were ever invoked. The Peace Palace, as solid as the world seemed, rose at The Hague. "In the twentieth century war will be dead," wrote Victor Hugo. It was, also, "impossible," so closely were the great powers economically intertwined and interdependent.

To be sure, in the first article in the first issue of *The Yale Review,* entitled simply "War," Professor William Graham Sumner took issue with this optimistic analysis, and with a good many other views then current. In his customary blunt, didactic way Professor Sumner fired his blast: ". . . the social philosophy of the modern civilized world is saturated with humanitarianism and flabby sentimentalism. . . . the reading public is led to suppose that the world is advancing along some line which they call 'progress' towards peace and brotherly love. Nothing could be more mistaken. . . . Can peace be universal? There is no reason to believe it."

Nevertheless, reason or no reason, Anglo-American opinion did believe it and acted accordingly. To the young, white, American male, life beckoned invitingly. The hazards, of which he was hardly aware, lay chiefly in sub-microscopic organisms which could cut off life, in alcohol, and in the lottery of marriage. But these were traps for others. For him success and position were almost certainly the rewards of hard work, a modicum of virtue and discretion, and a little luck.

Not only was the world safe, stable, and predictable, but so was his own life. No monstrous maelstrom could whirl up out of nowhere, with no rational cause, to demolish his whole environment, his every hope and prospect, even his and his nation's life. To be sure, Lincoln Steffens was writing of *The Shame of the Cities;* Henry Nevinson, of the deeper shame of slavery and the slave trade in Africa; but these and other manifest imperfections were regarded as the vestigial remains of past evils which mere exposure would end forever.

The first decade of the twentieth century was the Indian summer of the nineteenth. Surely a visitor from another planet, who knew nothing of our seasons, could not be blamed if, after the warmth and beauty of Indian summer, he was amazed and shocked by the onslaught of a New England winter. So it was in July 1914, in the town of Norfolk, Connecticut, where the present writer was spending the summer. The morning gathering in the post office, picking up the New York papers with the mail, delayed hardly a moment to note the murder of an Austrian Archduke and his wife at Sarajevo. It had nothing to do with them; off they went—the young men and the young women, too—to the engagements of their stable lives in a stable world.

Even as the days passed with their ultimatums, diplomatic moves, and mobilization orders, the group lingered only long enough to assure one another that war was impossible. The *New York Times* said so flatly on July 28: "That [war] is too dreadful for imagining and because it is too dreadful it cannot happen." The silly word "unthinkable" had not yet been invented; but, if it had been, war would have been "unthinkable." Then, as Lincoln said fifty years earlier, the war came.

It came; it destroyed; and it passed. With its passing a world order passed also—the world order of the nineteenth century, perhaps the most universal and impressive which this globe will see. The seven empires of Europe—the British, French, German, Russian, Austro-Hungarian, Ottoman, and Italian—guided, if they did not control, the course of events throughout the world. Their "concert" was maintaind by skilful shifts of British weight to maintain the semblance of a balance of power; and by a French diplomacy which compensated in brilliance and effectiveness for a decline in French power. For power was moving eastward in Europe, from France, which for a time won and held the hegemony of Europe, to Germany, which would have done so had not American power been thrown into the scales. It was soon to move farther eastward still.

All this, however, was not yet apparent. When the first issue of *The Yale Review* appeared, it was upon the tranquil and stable scene of the nineteenth century. For a hundred years international war had been held to a minimum; economic and technological progress in the century then just ending had exceeded that of the whole prior history of man; and the existence of one world had been achieved as never before or since. People, goods, and ideas moved about with an unequaled freedom, and the lives of people everywhere were molded by a gigantic, world-wide scheme.

All of this collapsed with the collapse of the empires which had made it possible. The Austro-Hungarian, German, Ottoman, and Czarist Russian empires were swept away by the First World War; the British, French, and Italian, by the Second and its aftermath. A world order ended.

Amid the ruins two great new powers faced one another. They were new powers; though, as states go, they were old states—older than Germany, Italy, or the British Empire. The future would depend on what their purposes and their relationship would be. Even before the war ended a discerning eye could see that their purposes were divergent and that their relationship would be hostile. Stalin's speech of February, 1946, left no doubt that this was the way he saw the situation and that he would act accordingly. So long, therefore, as each of the great new powers retained, or maintained, its power, there would no longer be one world order, but two. Furthermore, the centers of these two world orders would be in continued and protracted conflict. Instead of universal peace and universal law, the stage was set for universal revolutionary disorder and the reign of force and violence on a scale never yet dreamed of.

Such was the forecast of the new era drawn from the nature of the forces which were shaping it. But the minds of people are sometimes harder to change than their environment, perhaps, in part, because some changes in the environment cannot be seen and, therefore, do not seem real. Then, too, changes can be made difficult to observe when different things, ideas, or institutions are called by old and familiar names—democracy, freedom, peaceful, the people's will, coexistence, and so on. As a result, the nineteenth-century mind and nineteenth-century attitudes continue long after the environment which gave rise to them has vanished, just as the manner, titles, and behavior of the *ancien régime* continued in the *Conciergerie*.

Perhaps the chief point at which many minds have not grasped the essentials of our present environment is in this matter of the end of the one world of the nineteenth century. The idea of a world-wide consensus moved by Progress and Perfectibility toward peace, the rule of law and abolition of even the means of force, persists like plants without roots which draw their nourishment from the air. It persists not only as a haven for escape from the terrifying harshness of our times, but because it suits the purposes of leaders in both worlds to offer it as an achievable goal. This is a cruel hoax. There is no such consensus; there is, in fact, the exact opposite, an unbridgeable conflict.

"The essence of the rule of law ideal," writes Professor Stone in *Foreign Affairs* (July 1961), "lies, therefore, not in 'law' narrowly defined, but rather in the supremacy of certain ethical convictions, certain rules of decency prevalent in the community, and in the fact that those who are at the apex of power share those convictions and feel bound to conform to them.

93

# This Vast External Realm

A duly enacted statute to liquidate the Opposition would violate the 'rule of law' not (as it were) because it wasn't 'law,' but because it wasn't 'cricket.' "

From the U.S.S.R. and China to the Congo and Cuba this "rule of cricket" is not accepted, and in consequence the Opposition—the counter-revolutionary—is liquidated. There are no "rules of decency" prevalent in the world community, because there is no world community. There are two communities with antithetical conceptions of decency. We only deceive ourselves when we talk about "world peace through world law."

From this central self-deception others follow. The chief of these is that the instrumentalities of the rule of law are international organizations in various fields, a group of world legislatures on the one hand, and, on the other, binding, impartial, third-party adjudication ranging from the International Court of Justice to ceasefire or nuclear test ban commissions. Here Mr. Khrushchev has done his best to disillusion even the most deeply self-deceived. By his growing insistence on the "troika" principle—the tripartite veto on rule-making, investigation, and adjudication—he is pointing out, not, as he states it, that there are no neutrals between the Communist world and the free world, but that there are no common ethical principles or rules of decency between them. Here Mr. Khrushchev is nearly candid and wholly right.

Another fruit of self-deception as to the nature of our times is, as Professor Stone says,

The tendency . . . to condemn as wicked that kind of power which manifests itself in the launching of military force across the frontier of another state, and to leave all other kinds of power to work themselves out substantially uncontrolled. . . . The crucial question is whether there is the slightest chance that states will conform to a legal order of which this is virtually the only effective rule. In the absence of collective remedial action by the United Nations, must members submit to all kinds of illegality, injustice, and inhumanity as long as these do not take the specific form of an "armed attack" across a frontier? . . . Such an organization could only become a protective shield for those states whose predatory and imperial interests can be sufficiently realized without the need for "armed attack" across frontiers, and whose plaintive motto when the injured party reacts is: "You are a very wicked animal: when we attack you, you defend yourself."

The British, despoiled in Egypt, as we have been in Cuba, were pilloried for attempting to defend their rights under international law. Khrushchev says to us plainly that he plans to use the same technique again to deny the Western Allies their rights of access to Berlin. By the sleight of hand of a treaty with his puppet East German state, he claims that these can be ended. If we think otherwise and continue to exercise them, we become aggressors in his strange logic. "The Soviet Union and our friends do not want war and we will not start it. But we will defend our sovereignty, will fulfill our sacred duty to defend our freedom and independence. If any country violates peace and crosses the borders—ground, air, or water—of another it will assume full responsibility for the consequences of the aggression and will receive a proper rebuff."

But unhappily this strange logic is not only Khrushchev's. We invented it ourselves, and we can expect that an enforcement of our rights, in the only way they can be enforced in this dual world, by arms, will find many of our own citizens joining in the Soviet-inspired clamor before the United Nations for a cease-fire. In other words, we shall be urged in the name of law to cease enforcing our rights which cannot otherwise be rights. No wonder that this doctrine has led to the general breakdown of whatever respect for international law survived the nineteenth century.

Confusion about the nature of the world in which we live would be no more than the inevitable lag in appreciating a change in our environment, if the change were not a vital one and if the lack of understanding were not a serious handicap to our surviving the change. Doubtless a good many of our remote ancestors were slow to grasp the implications of the coming of the Ice Age. Those who were too slow probably do not have descendants. Today those who continue to live in the nineteenth century and devote their energies to advocating and acting upon its one world conceptions confuse, distract, and hamper efforts to meet the wholly new problems of survival and growth in a divided world.

The purpose of the United States in this divided world is simple to state and most difficult to accomplish. It is to maintain and strengthen an environment in which free societies can survive and flourish. The United States is not strong enough to do this alone. Furthermore, because of the very nature of a free society—that is, being free to make its own decisions—no nation, however strong, could do this alone. A nation cannot be coerced or bribed into wanting the benefits and accepting the burdens which go with a free society.

Nevertheless, strength is still needed because, without it, the Soviet bloc would impose its system by force, as it has done in Eastern Europe, upon people attempting to develop in their own way. The free environment must be defended by military power adequate to check this coercion. Economic strength is needed, too. For the free environment must be an environment of hope, offering opportunity of material development to those willing to learn and work.

All of this means that the free portion of a divided world must be criss-crossed by innumerable cooperative arrangements, freely entered into and purposefully led. These arrangements must be consistent with one another, not contradictory. It must also be understood that some things are more important than others. All ideas are not created free and equal.

The indispensable collaborator of the United States in providing security and opportunity for the free world is Western Europe. Geography, history, population, resources, and technology all combine to make this so. Working together these two areas have twice the population and three times the productive capacity of the Soviet Union, an ample base for military defense and economic development. But if the Soviet Union should be able to control the production of Europe, our problems would soon be beyond our capacity to deal with them.

It is all too easy to lose sight of this vital truth, or never to see it at all. We are, and should be, deeply concerned with social, political, and economic development in Latin America, Asia, and Africa. In all of these areas revolutionary movements are pressing hard for change and improvement. In many of them independence has been wrested from weakened colonial powers by people wholly incompetent to manage their own affairs and, therefore, in desperate need of disinterested help and instruction.

It is often said, sometimes within the United States Government itself, that our interests in the alliance with Europe and in the undeveloped areas are competing and conflicting. This is the opposite of the truth; only the North American–Western European connection makes possible the development of Latin American, Asian, and African countries in security and in an environment which leaves them freedom of choice to develop in their own way. In some cases memories of a colonial past feed suspicion; in others, the liquidation of remaining colonial relations may bring conflict and brutalities. But both only obscure an essential truth.

The essential truth is that the hope of the whole free world, developed and undeveloped nations alike, lies in the ever closer association and economic growth of Western Europe and North America. For in that economic growth—impossible without common institutions to harmonize economies which deeply affect one another—lie expanding capabilities to deal with the needs of growing populations at home, the export of capital goods for development abroad, and the provision for military defense.

There is not, as many liberals appear to think, an inevitable dichotomy between our interest in our NATO partners and in the undeveloped countries. One writer, for instance, recently approved of the United States' "supporting the U.N. resolution to investigate conditions in Portuguese Angola, thereby abandoning the concept that the United States must always cater to allied sensibilities, whether that enhances United States long-range interests or not; . . ." Here the tendentious use of color phrases—"always cater to allied sensibilities"—points to "judgments and institutions," in Justice Holmes's phrase, "more subtle than any articulate major premise." The "thereby" clause gives away the emotional basis for approving our vote. It was not because our support "thereby" caused the resolution to be adopted (since it failed of adoption), or because, if adopted, the investigation would have taken place, or because, if investigation should take place, conditions in Angola would be improved. What our voting for the resolution signified to the writer was wholly negative. We signified "thereby" the abandonment of an attitude toward an ally which he describes contemptuously as catering to sensibilities "whether that enhances United States long-range interests or not." His intuition is against supporting an ally in a colonial controversy, as a matter of policy. Indeed it goes further than this. He is against supporting such an ally "whether that enhances United States long-range interests or not." In other words we are to abandon our ally even if doing so impairs our long-range interests.

The person who posed such an issue was not concerned with consequences but with attitudes. To him the possibility of weakening an essential alliance and losing an invaluable military asset is "to cater to allied sensibilities," while a futile vote is "supporting a U.N. resolution" (in fact a Liberian resolution), which carries a connotation of beneficial result. Here we see the assumption that our national acts should be designed to lead to—or square us with—some consensus which will in itself determine events. There is no realization of the struggle in our divided world, of the tragic consequences of reckless, emotional, or impulsive handling of a vital asset, of the grave danger of becoming victims of a public diplomacy concerned with the "images" created by words and postures without regard to constructive achievement.

The United States is a great power with global responsibilities and innumerable connections. It is intolerable that the United States should be required to vote on every resolution, however theoretical, however hostile to one of its close allies, which any country may regard as useful in a propaganda campaign. Of course, the responsibilities of leadership inevitably draw the United States into matters not of direct concern to it when they affect the whole alliance and the whole free world. But its influence can be made infinitely more effective by quiet, private, and friendly action than by public posturing as a friend of the oppressed and the voice of conscience. The latter does not help the objects of help because it makes concessions much more difficult, and the "image" sought for continues only so long as this progressive alienation of friends continues to weaken the alliance.

It is just this sort of illusory ambition to be leaders of world opinion—when there is no world conscience —which opens the way for the unending Communist bloc effect to divide the alliance, weaken the free world, and make even more difficult the process—painful enough at best—of the transition of peoples from a colonial to a self-governing status. It makes difficult, too, the continued solidarity of the North American– Western European connection united in purpose to provide military defense against Communist encroachment and economic opportunity in the community of the free world.

In other ways the nineteenth century contributes to the difficulty of the tasks which the twentieth poses for the free world. Sometimes yearning for national power and prestige stands in the way of European integration, as "national sovereignty" in financial and trade matters impedes Atlantic economic integration.

## This Vast External Realm

The same notions of unbridled sovereignty are strangely joined with peremptory demands on industrialized states by undeveloped countries for economic help. Rights without obligations, funds without knowledge or plans of how to use them, the idea that material prosperity through self-development is evidence of guilt, that foreign investment is exploitation only expiated by expropriation—all these doctrines are the offspring of this union wherever it has occurred from Asia to the Caribbean.

In the nation which must give leadership in the strengthening of the free world, if any is to be given, many turn from the task in discouragement or disgust. They weary of the unending burden of foreign aid in all its aspects, trade policies for new conditions, military necessities, and the adjustments which every nation must make to national and parochial attitudes of others. Discouragement and disgust are in themselves evidences that those experiencing them have never understood their present environment or its problems. These are the emotions of disillusion engendered by expecting the world of "Locksley Hall" and finding oneself amid the flotsam and jetsam of the old world upon the shores of the new.

We shall be faced—and soon—with a confrontation which will call for all the courage, resourcefulness, strength, and steadiness we can summon. We cannot escape from it into the rhetoric of the last century, or find guidance in abstractions or general moral principles, or in emotional exhortation. A romantic and outdated conception of the world and peoples around us will surely lead to disaster. One cannot exaggerate what is at stake as the days shorten in 1961. It will be a pity if our knowledge, skill, and wisdom do not approximate our risks. Such, unhappily, was the case fifty years ago.

# Real and Imagined Handicaps of Our Democracy in the Conduct of Its Foreign Relations

Much has been said in the post-war period about the handicaps and defects of a democracy in facing the challenge of dictatorships and totalitarian states. Perhaps this afternoon we might look into this matter a little bit. I am persuaded that there are handicaps. Some of them are real and have to be faced, and some of them could quite easily be remedied if we

This address was given by former Secretary of State Dean Acheson at the Harry S. Truman Library, Independence, Missouri, on March 31, 1962. The occasion was the unveiling of a portrait bust of Mr. Acheson, executed by Miss Eleanor Platt of New York City, and donated to the Library by a group of his friends headed by former Secretary of the Interior Oscar L. Chapman.

chose to do that. We might, perhaps, look at these together and see which is which.

First I want to read to you something written a
hundred and thirty years ago by a man who knew a
great deal about democracies. He was Alexis de Tocqueville, who, speaking of democracies and foreign
policy, wrote this:

> Foreign politics demand scarcely any of those qualities
> which are peculiar to a democracy; they require, on the
> contrary, the perfect use of almost all those in which it
> is deficient. Democracy is favorable to the increase of the
> internal resources of a state; it diffuses wealth and com-
> fort, promotes public spirit, and fortifies the respect for
> law in all classes of society; all these are advantages
> which have only an indirect influence over the relations
> which one people bears to another. But a democracy
> can only with great difficulty regulate the details of an
> important undertaking, persevere in a fixed design, and
> work out its execution in spite of serious obstacles. It
> cannot combine its measures with secrecy or await their
> consequences with patience. These are qualities which
> more especially belong to an individual or an aristoc-
> racy; and they are precisely the qualities by which a
> nation, like an individual, attains a dominant position.

Now that was a pretty acute observation by a man
writing a hundred and thirty years ago. I think we
can say that most of what de Tocqueville wrote is still
true. I think that we may add that some of it can perhaps be questioned. I think that we have to say further
that a good deal more has to be said. Just to start off,
is it altogether true that "only with great difficulty"

can a democracy "regulate the details of an important undertaking, persevere in a fixed design, and work out its execution in spite of serious obstacles?"

I submit that that is open to doubt, and as an illustration that it is open to doubt, I would like to suggest the great measures which were taken by a former President of the United States, Mr. Harry S. Truman, in his two administrations following the war. Now these were pursuant to a great design. They were executed with skill. All those measures were designed to create a new world, which later on I shall speak about a little more, a new world out of the remains of a very broken one, to build up the strength which was necessary to defend that world, to bring hope and opportunity to people who did not have hope or opportunity. This was a great design and it was well worked out even to the details. Perhaps de Tocqueville overstated the case in this respect.

As to perseverance, we had better wait a little before we boast. The United States has been barely fifteen years at work upon this effort and many people are tired of it already. We hear from Congress moans of anguish about some of the burdens we have undertaken and it may be that de Tocqueville will turn out to be right, that it is very difficult for democracy to persevere. But, at any rate, we begin to see a ray of hope. The picture is not quite as black as he painted it.

When we come to secrecy I can't offer you much hope. We regard secrecy as a sin. "Secret diplomacy" are words of opprobrium. Another phrase which we look on with great doubt is "behind closed doors." I had always thought that the very conception of a door was that it might be closed; but apparently it is wrong to close one in the domain of diplomacy.

Of patience, we have very little indeed; and I think that this lack of patience comes from several of our most beloved clichés. We delight to say to one another, that our soldiers win the war on the battlefield and our statesmen lose the peace at the conference table. This is a pleasant thing to say because one likes soldiers and dislikes diplomats. Therefore, it puts each in his proper place. But it seems to me that it comes from a basic misunderstanding of the very nature of force.

Force can do some things and it can't do other things. This is what is not understood in this cliché. Force can overcome other force. This is its only achievement. If one has greater force than the enemy, that force can be overcome. There is then a beaten and defeated enemy. What happens at this point? Here force becomes quite a useless weapon in the hands of a democracy. A democracy cannot use force as a dictatorship can, to crush a defeated enemy and force him to accept an alien rule and an alien dictatorship. It isn't in the nature of a democracy to accept that sort of burden. The British thought for years they could do it in Ireland; and again they thought they could do it in India; and the French thought they could do it in Algeria. The trouble was not that they did not have enough force; but that they couldn't, in consonance with their own conscience, with the inner life and ethical standards of a democracy, use their force for that purpose.

# This Vast External Realm

Almost at the moment of victory, the moment arms have been stricken from the hands of a defeated enemy, a wholly new situation occurs—a situation where force is of little importance, and where we are returned to the basic processes of democracy itself—to win the consent of the defeated enemy in a new endeavor, to the mutual benefit of both victor and vanquished. This, indeed, was the great achievement of the Truman Administration. The achievement was not to regard Germany and Japan as enemies but to regard them immediately as the subjects of reconstruction, to change their attitudes, to restore their broken economies and their disrupted societies, so that they might both begin to become members of a world order. And so it seems to me that here again there is a possibility of hope.

The possibility of patience begins once a democracy understands what it is trying to do. Impatient people coin a wonderful phrase, "We must wage peace just as soldiers wage war until we smash through to victory." This is ridiculous talk. You cannot wage peace in a forceful and vigorous way. You cannot smash people into being good or being good citizens of the world. All these ideas are alien ideas. Therefore, once a democracy begins to understand what it is that it is trying to achieve, it may be patient in waiting for consequences which cannot occur overnight.

Perhaps, too, a democracy can help itself by revising its institutions so there is an opportunity for patience. I have often talked with President Truman about the problem presented by the frequency of elections to the

House of Representatives, and to one-third of the Senate. If voters have to appraise the work of Congress every two years, there is not much room for patience. Congress can hardly enact substantial measures and get results from them in two years. Legislation is a hard crop to plant, and one cannot expect to harvest it before it has sprouted. Therefore, it would be wise, if democracy is to learn patience, to have institutions which make patience possible.

I have endeavored to put a democracy's difficulties in dealing with foreign policy into the two categories which I have mentioned before. Those that one can hope to remedy; others, which one must live with— the deeper ones, the ones that go to the very nature of democracy in any land, or to the very nature of our institutions in this land, when they are confronted with a conflict which was never anticipated.

First of all let me take two illustrations of handicaps which could be cured without too much difficulty. They are taken from the role of the Congress in relation to foreign affairs. These illustrations are not inherent in the system. They aren't the result of law. They are merely the result of inertia. One of them is the wholly fortuitous result of the seniority principle as applied to the committees of the House and of the Senate. Here the wayward personality is extolled to its most unhappy apotheosis. Mere chance, not party action, not the healthy back and forth fight of parties, but mere chance, brings somebody into a position of power who has a particular prejudice which he cannot or will not surmount. As a result the whole work of

Congress is made infinitely harder than it has to be, because somebody is where he shouldn't be. He might be excellent in another place, but in this place he is not, and yet the seniority rule produces this result. It makes impossible, for instance, something which Presidents of both parties have wanted to bring about, a long-term financing of foreign aid, instead of appropriations for only twelve months at a time.

Another matter, of this same sort, coming out of this same field, the role of the Congress, is the practice which has grown up through no requirement in the Constitution, no requirement in law—of having annual appropriations and annual authorizations for most of the important programs of government. Now this is a sheer obstacle race. This is just making it hard for ourselves, for no purpose. Actually Congress wants to retain more control over the executive, by this interminable squirrel-in-the-cage activity, than it's entitled to retain. Four times a year important members of the government, any number of their assistants, any number of members of Congress, have to listen to the same speeches. One can wake up in the middle of the night and make these speeches after a while, and often does. Day after day after day. The time of the Congress, the time of the Executive, the time of the press, the time of all sorts of important employees of the government is taken up by merely reciting over and over and over again the same words. I've often thought, with envy, of a Buddhist prayer wheel. If we could just put something up and turn it by hand to satisfy these people it would seem to me to be important. This is something which could be cured. It isn't inherent in the American system. To cure it would not bring about a dictatorship. It would merely let us act like ordinary sensible human beings.

Another handicap we can correct is the tribute which is levied by the fourth and fifth estates for performing their essential duty in a democracy. The fourth estate we're all familiar with; that, of course, is the press. The fifth estate is the radio and the television.

Now, clearly it's essential that our Chief of State and Government, the President, should have direct contact with the people of the United States. To do that he must have the cooperation of the media of communications. There's only one President in recent times, that I know of, who could get on a train and go around and talk to everybody in the United States; but he had a lot of energy. Therefore, he needs the press, he needs the radio, he needs television to help him. The people have to have information.

This is a democracy, and a democracy is different from a representative form of government. This country can't go any faster than the people are willing to go and they have to have information; they have to have education in what this information means. Data don't explain themselves. Data are too complicated today. Information has to be explained. This requires education.

The President is the chief educator in the United States. You remember, I think it was Lord Sherbrooke, after the Reform Act of 1867, who said, "We must educate our masters." Our masters are the people of the United States. They must be educated. James Wilson spoke about this in a very telling way before the Pennsylvania Constitutional Ratifying Convention in 1787. Here are the words which are infinitely true today. He said: "There is a remedy for every distemper in government, if the people are not wanting to themselves. For a people wanting to themselves, there is no remedy: from their power . . . there is no appeal; to their error, there is no superior principle of correction."

The people will be wanting to themselves if they do not understand the world in which they live; and education, the capability of understanding something as complicated as that, is not found in the state of nature. The mode by which this is brought about is effort. Therefore, there is a vast field in which the fourth and fifth estates must cooperate. But they exact a tribute for doing so which is unnecessary and exorbitant.

This tribute is in the form of the unorganized, irresponsible, and downright dangerous press conferences to which the President of the United States and his Secretary of State are subjected. This is done in no other country in the world. I don't mean the press conference is not held, but not the anarchic press conference which is held in the United States of America. And it comes about, I think, from a combination of reasons for which the press, the radio, the television, and public officials are all responsible. The press, the television, the radio on their side want to have a show. They are after spot news. They hope the

President will make a mistake or the Secretary of State will make a mistake. If he has a slip of the tongue, if he says, as General Marshall did once, Russia when he meant England, this mixes things up in a perfectly magnificent way and cables flash around the world and a lot of papers are sold.

On the other hand, very often, public officials want to use the press, the radio, and the television for their own purposes. They believe they're smarter than the press. They believe they can use it for advertising. A very great President, now dead, gave momentum to this sort of use, which was a misfortune then and has remained so since. When the press starts to do this the radio and television say, "We must come in too." So, these officials with tremendous burdens on their shoulders are treated like quiz-kids. They are faced with questions of which they have no notice. To be sure, they all go through a sort of drill beforehand in which employees think up the silliest questions which could possibly be asked and devise answers. But, this is an unnecessary handicap and it's something which should not be done.

One more self-imposed handicap and then I will mention a few much more serious things. This is the political appointment to represent the United States in foreign countries, a very curious survival. It comes, I think, because we just don't think about it. We know, obviously, that in every walk of life the means used to do something affect the nature of the thing done. Obviously, tools available a hundred years ago, materials available a hundred years ago produced certain types of architecture. Different tools available today, different materials, produce a wholly different type of architecture. The means available affect the results obtained. Or take communication. A quill pen produces one type of communication. If one has a typewriter, shorthand, a secretary, a telephone, radio, telegraph, they produce a different type of communication and affect the substance of the communication itself. In the twentieth century we do not have letters like those of Horace Walpole or papers as thoughtful as the Federalist Papers. One writes better and thinks more carefully with a pen in one's own hand. Dictation and copies in quintuplicate are the curse of modern government.

So it is in the world of diplomacy. Everywhere else we think professionalism or at least long training is important. One does not go to a doctor who thought only the day before that he'd like to practice medicine. Everywhere we want people trained in what they are to do. In diplomacy, also, we need professionalism. Of course, here there is room for people who are not, in the technical sense, career diplomats; although many of these people—take Mr. David Bruce for instance—are professionals in diplomacy, in everything except having their names on the list of career officers.

Or if one is looking for unique quality—if one, for instance, had to find almost a pro-consul to take over the control of Germany after military government ended—then one may do well to look for that unusual combination of qualities which, for instance, was found in Mr. John J. McCloy. But for the main run of diplomatic representation we need and want professionals. I hasten to add that I think a higher percentage of chiefs of mission were career men at the end of Mr. Truman's administration than ever before or since.

The appointment of political ambassadors is based on illusions. One of these illusions is that this is a good and cheap way of raising campaign funds. It is neither good because it doesn't raise very much, nor is it cheap because it has produced costly results.

The second illusion is that the political officers are competent. This is perhaps the greatest illusion of all. They are not competent and they fall victim to the chief error to which an ambassador can fall victim. As one Prime Minister plaintively pointed out, "The United States sends a man to me who is supposed to be their ambassador to my country, but who insists on becoming my ambassador to his country." This practice of adopting the country to which one is accredited is a very grave weakness.

The third illusion is that a political appointment pleases the politicians and solidifies the machine. I think it creates more resentment among the disappointed than it ever creates satisfaction among the rewarded. Here is a self-created handicap to which we do not need to subject ourselves.

Now let me speak for a few moments about some much deeper handicaps, those which come from the very essence of democracy or from the nature of our own institutions of which we are justly proud. The first one I want to lay before you is the greater difficulty of achieving discipline when it must be self-imposed rather than imposed by someone else. A democracy must discipline itself. A dictatorship disciplines its people.

Take, for example, the extreme difficulty of a democracy disciplining itself sufficiently to maintain an adequate part of its citizenry in the Armed Forces. This is not anything new to America, or to Britain, or to France, or to any other modern democracy. Or to an ancient one; it was a problem in Athens. The Athenians never could solve it; and the Spartans could. Here is a very great handicap. No government in the United States could possibly have prevented the demobilization of our twelve million men after the Second World War. However, the Soviet Union was able to prevent the demobilization of its forces; so when it was necessary to withdraw American troops both from Europe and from the Far East, a handicap was created for the democracies which did not exist for the dictatorship. General Marshall used to say the ups and downs of American military policy created difficulties which could be obviated if we could only maintain a sensible mean. We had a vast "down" from forty-six to fifty; then an "up" during the Korean crisis from fifty to fifty-three; then a "down" again between fifty-three and sixty-two; and now we are in a period of "up." This is one of the difficulties which are almost inherent in the nature of a democracy: the inability of a community to discipline itself so that it consistently says, "Even though the danger is not as apparent today as it was last year, we will still have a steady military policy."

# Real and Imagined Handicaps

The next problem comes from the immense difficulty which all modern democracies have today in understanding the nature of the world in which they live.
Why is this so hard? In the first place, because the
problem is hard. In the second place, because understanding when it comes is so harsh that the mind re-
jects it.

Let us look at the first for a moment. What is the
nature of our time? We live at a time when a unique
period in the history of the world has come to an end.
This period we may roughly call the nineteenth century, a hundred years of stability, blest by the absence,
to a very large extent, of international war, a century
of greater economic progress than in the entire history
of man from the discovery of the wheel to 1800, and
when there was "one world" more than there ever had
been before or there ever will be again in our lifetime.

In the nineteenth century, people, ideas, and goods
moved more freely throughout the world than they
have before or since. Why? Because after the Republican and Napoleonic Wars, due to the wise peace that
was made, and due to the experience of that vast struggle, the great empires of Europe with their colonial
possessions created a balance of power and a truly
wide order, or system. The great empires, the British,
the French, the German, the Russian, the Austro-
Hungarian, the Ottoman stretched over almost all the
world either directly or in the areas which they influenced. And this created the peace, this made possible
the economic progress, this made possible the "one
world."

# This Vast External Realm

All the time that quiet was being enjoyed, much was going on under the surface; power was moving to the East in Europe. Whereas in 1814 it required the whole power of Europe to contain the power of France, in 1914 the entire power of Europe was not capable of controlling the power of Germany; and twice the United States intervened to do so.

What do we mean by power? We mean a combination of resources, of population, of technology, and of will which affects and is respected by surrounding societies. This thing called power was moving out of France, where it has been for two hundred years, into Germany, and has now moved out of Germany into Soviet Russia, presenting the question of whether a combination of other available power in the world is able to balance it. This change is the dominant factor in determining the nature of our times. The old "one world" is gone. There are two worlds; they are antithetical worlds. This is hard for us to grasp. It is hard for us to grasp that this other power group of powers, this other half of the world, is so revolutionary and hostile to every conception of our constitutional order that there cannot be for many, many years, perhaps several generations, the sort of world that the nineteenth century was, and out of which have come most of our ideas.

We are nineteenth century people. Our minds are our great, great grandmothers' and fathers' minds. We aren't twentieth-century people. Our ideas are inherited ideas. Let me take one with which to illustrate my point.

# Real and Imagined Handicaps

We hear a great deal of talk about the pursuit of world peace through world law as a practicable current policy for this country. But is this a tenable policy for our time? What do we mean when we talk about law; what do we mean when we talk about world law? The Chief Justice will bear with me if I suggest that underlying the law which he has to administer, the law which comes from the Constitution of the United States, the law which comes from the Acts of Congress, and the law which comes from the decisions of courts, there are the basic ethical conceptions of a society. These are the foundations of the kind of law which permit third-party adjudication, that is, it permits the court to decide a dispute between the two people with their acquiescence. Why do people say, "We accept this as the right way to settle our dispute"? Because, underlying the law is a common ethical consideration. Why does the British Parliament not enact a law making the Labour Party unconstitutional? Not because it wouldn't be law. Anything the British Parliament enacts is a law. There isn't any other power to review it. It isn't because it isn't within the law. It's because, as a legal scholar has written, the British wouldn't consider it "cricket." It would run counter to a basic ethical concept. They do not play the game that way.

Now, is there a basic ethical concept between what we call the "free world" and what we call the "Communist world"? The answer is that there is not. Every conception of ours is regarded as spurious, ridiculous, weak, or foolish by the Communist world, and every conception of theirs seems to us basically immoral and horrible. Therefore, when you hear talk of world law, ask yourself whether it is possible that the Soviet Union and the United States could conceivably agree on the underlying principles which some court could administer or from which some joint body could legislate. This is too far away to furnish a basis for a practicable policy. It is a nineteenth-century conception, not a twentieth-century one.

Our times are divided times, in which power looms large and in which force is only a little way off from the controversies of the moment. But such ideas are too harsh a result for people to accept. They make the outlook too dangerous, too bleak. So the mind reaches out for hope, and some people find hope in the possibility of a Chino-Soviet conflict. Can't we drive a wedge between the Chinese and the Russians? Some people find hope in a sort of messianic United Nations which mystically, out of weakness, can produce strength. Some people believe that there is a magic wand called negotiation; that if you just negotiate, things happen which they really know can't happen. And some people feel that fear is the big hope. Fear of nuclear war will prevent all these dangers from happening. So a babel of voices is turned loose on our democracy. Pundits in the press, political leaders, writers, clerics, everybody is saying something to our democracy and the confusion is almost complete.

I suggest that there are only three possible responses to the nature of our time. One is to oppose Russian purposes until it becomes clear to the Russians that these purposes are unachievable and have to be abandoned. That course of action calls for "Cold War." The second one is to accept Russian purposes and to say, "I would rather be Red than dead." This course is called by the Russians "peaceful coexistence." The third course is for one world to try to destroy the other. This is "Hot War." This is nuclear war. Now I believe that the only sensible course is the first course.

One may say, "Of course you come to that conclusion by the way you stated the question." But it isn't I who stated the question. This is the way the Russians have stated the question. What do they mean by negotiation? Here again is a situation where we are remaining in the nineteenth century. To us, negotiation is a method adopted by two people each of whom has already decided that he would rather settle a difference than not settle it, and hence will make concessions. To the Russians, a negotiation is a way of continuing a controversy. They don't want to settle it. They want to gain an advantage. To them negotiation is an instrument of the Cold War, not a method of ending the Cold War.

I suggest that a candid mind must come to the conclusion that the only response to the nature of the time is, as I said a moment ago, to continue the Cold War. It must reject the other possibilities, preventive war and acceptance of Russian purposes.

It is not easy for us in this room to analyze the problem and come to a conclusion. But it is infinitely harder for a hundred and eighty million of us living in the United States under the institutions which we love and of which we are proud. Our very size and our cherished institutions add to the problem of reaching a consensus which is hard even for a small country, as the Dutch have learned in wrestling with the problem of New Guinea, and the Belgians with that of the Congo. For a hundred and eighty million people to figure out the necessities and the direction of leadership in a world as divided and as confused as this is immensely more difficult. It is the difference between handling an ocean liner and a launch.

Then, too, the tools with which this democracy has to work, the institutions inherent in our Constitutional order, with its insistence upon the separation of governmental powers, are not handy for working on foreign affairs. As Justice Brandeis pointed out a good many years ago, the separation of power was not intended to create governmental efficiency or harmony. It was intended to create conflict. Those who wrote the Constitution thought—and I believe rightly thought —that to prevent tyranny, conflict between the powers in government would be likely to keep each within its proper place.

Europe furnished them with examples of personal tyranny, and classical history with tyrannies of popular assemblies. They could see too, that a Supreme Court might, unless it was checked by the powers of the Executive and the Legislative, take over too commanding a position. So these powers were put in the position of checking one another in what we call the system of Checks and Balances. This system does exactly what it was intended to do. What was not foreseen was that when foreign affairs become predominant in the survival of the state, and where foreign affairs are carried on in the sort of world conflict short of war which I've been talking about, what one needs is harmony within the government and not conflict.

We see this when war breaks out. The Constitution understood this. When war breaks out, there are both psychological and legal consequences which bring about harmony and unity within the country and the government rather than conflict. We all say, "Let's show the Kaiser," or "Let's show Hitler," or "Let's show Stalin," whoever it is, that the country is united behind the President and under the flag. This is a very fine thing and this happens. Then, the Constitution with its provisions for war powers makes it perfectly clear that the Federal Government is supreme in this realm and the state governments take a secondary place. It also becomes perfectly clear that among the three departments of government, both for legal and psychological reasons, the President has the supreme position. Congress in part gives it to him under the war power; the psychology of the nation makes it certain that he will exercise it and will not be opposed as long as we are all in grave danger.

Now we try in a way to carry this over into foreign policy in peacetime. We say, "Politics stops at the water's edge." This is supposed to mean that in matters of foreign policy the country is united. But it is a cliché and means nothing at all. The essence of foreign policy exists in the things which everybody agrees, and must agree, are the subject of partisan party conflict and between the powers of government. For instance, taxes have a great deal to do with foreign policy. So does trade policy. So do financial, budgetary, and agricultural policies, and so they gravely affect and are affected by foreign policy. But among all these subjects there is not and cannot be any place where politics stops. We have battles about foreign trade, and about taxes, and appropriations for foreign policy, about compulsory military service. We have battles as to whether the Air Force or the Army or the Navy should do this, that, or the other thing. All these matters which enter into and make foreign policy continue to be, under our system, the subject of conflict.

Now, I do not propose that the Constitution be changed. I am not criticizing the Constitution. I have taken more oaths to support it, in wartime and in peacetime, than almost anyone in the room except the Chief Justice and the President. Then why talk about it? Because the Constitutional final processes which govern the way in which we reach a consensus in this country profoundly affect the conduct of our foreign relations. Compared to an authoritarian state it takes us longer to reach a national view and we have more difficulty in maintaining it after we reach it.

But there is no reason for despair. One of the interesting things about the history of the United States is how highly controversial ideas, legislation, and programs become, after a time, entirely accepted. Today, the Sherman Law, which was the subject of vast controversy when it went into effect, is regarded as one of those things about which there can't be any conflict.

# Real and Imagined Handicaps

No party, in its right mind, would ever put in a plank saying, "We're for repeal of the Sherman Law." No party would advocate the repeal of the income tax; but in 1895, Mr. Joseph H. Choate, in arguing to the Supreme Court (successfully) against its constitutionality, declared it to be "communistic in its purposes and tendencies." Every one of the New Deal proposals of 1933, '34, '35 was regarded as the end of a free society in the United States. Social Security and the control of the securities market were the principal targets. Would anybody now propose to abolish either? Controversial proposals, once accepted, soon became hallowed.

If our leaders were to spend some time looking into the nature of our time, thinking about it deeply, and perhaps exercising some small degree of courage—leaders on all sides and in both parties—a consensus could move forward. Today, I read in the British press that "the British public have lost faith in politicians." This is apparently based on a belief that they speak out of both sides of their mouths. Why do people think this? I suggest it is because the times in which we live are so confusing, because the reports we get of them are so confusing, and the proposals so contradictory, that public men find themselves speaking different languages to many audiences at the same time. This is not conducive to education or leadership.

But, as the people gradually begin to understand, a very curious, almost inexplicable thing goes on in a democracy, the people become more critical. The leaders get a hint that the people have more sense than they thought they had. Leaders begin to talk with more sense; the people to understand better; and quickly, very quickly, a consensus begins to form. Once that starts an understanding of specific events becomes possible, and with that, action—action in this obscure and dangerous world where one must always act on premises imperfectly understood.

This is my analysis of the difficulties, the handicaps, of a democracy and of our democracy in the times in which we live. It is poor recompense for the honor and joy which have been brought to me today. But it is only by understanding the nature of our times and by facing its difficulties with a candid mind that we can give the values represented here in this Library the fullest opportunity to survive. Thank you very much.

# Ethics in International Relations Today

The discussion of ethics or morality in our relations with other states is a prolific cause of confusion. The righteous who seek to deduce foreign policy from ethical or moral principles are as misleading and misled as the modern Machiavellis who would conduct our foreign relations without regard to them.

Most of what we, and a good part of the non-Communist world, regard as ethical principles relates to conduct, the behavior of individuals toward one another. There is pretty general agreement that it is better to act straightforwardly, candidly, honorably, and courageously than duplicitously, conspiratorially, or treacherously. This is true of conduct toward friends and toward those who are ill-disposed to us. It is well

Lecture delivered at Amherst College, December 9, 1964.

127

that our government should give to foreigners as well as to our own people as clear an idea as possible of its intentions. To do so should inspire confidence and increase stability. One need not counsel perfection—for instance, to tell the whole truth—but it ought not to be too much to advise telling nothing but the truth, advice which might usefully have been given to President Eisenhower before he began issuing statements about the U-2 aircraft shot down some years ago over the Soviet Union.

The French school of diplomacy, founded by Cardinal Richelieu, the dominant school for nearly three centuries, and probably still the best ever devised, was based, as François de Callières stated, upon the principle that "open dealing is the basis of confidence" (a very different idea from President Wilson's ill-considered maxim, "open covenants openly arrived at"). He adds, "The negotiator therefore must be a man of probity and one who loves truth; otherwise he will fail to inspire confidence." And again, "Deceit is the measure of the smallness of mind of him who uses it . . . a lie always leaves behind it a drop of poison. . . . Menaces always do harm to negotiation. . . ."

It does not detract from the purity of his morals that he supports them with worldly wisdom:

> The diplomatist must be . . . a good listener, courteous, and agreeable. He should not seek to gain a reputation as a wit, nor should he be so disputatious as to divulge secret information in order to clinch an argument. Above all the good negotiator must possess enough self-control to resist the longing to speak before he has

thought out what he wants to say. . . . He should pay attention to women but never lose his heart . . . , possess the patience of a watch-maker . . . should not be given to drink . . . and be able to tell where, in any foreign country, the real sovereignty lies. . . . Finally . . . a good cook is often an excellent conciliator.

For any of you who are contemplating a career in the Foreign Service, François de Callières is as sound an adviser today as he was in 1716.

Without laboring the point further, I take it as clear that, where an important purpose of diplomacy is to further enduring good relations between states, the methods—the modes of conduct—by which relations between states are carried on must be designed to inspire trust and confidence. To achieve this result the conduct of diplomacy should conform to the same moral and ethical principles which inspire trust and confidence when followed by and between individuals.

The purpose of our own diplomacy, as of the French school, requires the inspiring of trust and confidence, for our governmental goal for many years has been to preserve and foster an environment in which free societies may exist and flourish. When we have said this, we had better stop and think before concluding that the policies which will advance us toward this goal can usefully be discussed or evaluated in terms of moral or ethical principles.

In the first place, a little reflection will convince us that the same conduct is not moral under all circumstances. Its moral propriety seems to depend, certainly in many cases, upon the relationship of those concerned with the conduct. For instance, parents have the moral right, indeed duty, to instill moral and religious ideas in their children and correct moral error. Ministers, priests, rabbis, and mullahs have much the same duties to their flocks, including that of correcting heresy, when they can make up their minds what it is.

But these same acts on the part of public officials—certainly in the United States—would be both wrong and a denial of the fundamental rights of the citizen. Indeed, even prayer prescribed and led by teachers in our public schools is condemned by our courts with the approval of some of our churches. The attempt of both governmental and religious bodies to censor literature, painting, sculpture, the theater, and the movies, under the aegis of those alliterative adjectives, lewd and lascivious, seems to me intolerable. Parents, if they are any good, can shield their children from whatever they choose. The rest of us had better take our chances with mortal sin, rather than to have policemen, trained to handle traffic and arrest criminals, become judges of what art we may see or read. And it is just as bad when the local watch-and-ward society or church body tries to do the same thing.

So, acts, moral in one human relationship, may become quite the reverse in another. Generally speaking, morality often imposes upon those who exercise the powers of government standards of conduct quite different from what might seem right to them as private citizens. For instance, the moral, and indeed the legal, duty of a judge in bringing to bear upon a party before him the coercive power of the state is not to do "what he thinks is right," or by his decision to mold the kind of society which seems to him to accord with divine will or high human aspiration. He has not been given this great power so that he might administer personal justice, even though his conscience be as clear as that of Harun al-Rashid or Henry the Second when they decided disputes by virtuous inspiration. Our courts are supposed to be courts of law; and whatever justice may be (I know of no satisfactory definition of it), it is to be achieved, as the phrase goes, "under law." It is our hope that the consciences of our judges will be guided, not by what they think is right, but what they believe the law requires them to decide, whether they like it or not.

So, too, what may be quite proper and moral for a private citizen—for instance, the pursuit of personal advantage, or the advantage of a group—often, and rightly, is condemned if done when he assumes legislative or executive office. This distinction is not always perceived and has gotten many people into trouble. Even a candidate for office cannot expect the same latitude given private individuals in exposing his ignorance and stupidity. November 3 last made that rather clear.

Moreover, the vocabulary of morals and ethics is inadequate to discuss or test foreign policies of states. We are told that what is ethical is characterized by what is excellent in conduct and that excellence may be judged by what is right and proper, as against what is wrong, by existing standards. But when we look for standards we find that none exist. What passes for ethical standards for governmental policies in foreign affairs is a collection of moralisms, maxims, and slogans, which neither help nor guide, but only confuse, decision on such complicated matters as the multilateral nuclear force, a common grain price in Europe, policy in Southeast Asia, or exceptions and disparities under the Kennedy Round of tariff negotiations.

One of the most often invoked and delusive of these maxims is the so-called principle of self-determination. In the continuing dispute over Cyprus it has been invoked by nearly all parties to the struggle to support whatever they were temporarily seeking to achieve—by all Cypriots to justify revolt against British rule, by Archbishop Makarios to support an independent government for the whole island, by Greek Cypriots as foundation for enosis (union) with Greece, and by Turkish Cypriots for partition of the island and double enosis, union of one part with Greece and the other with Turkey.

Despite its approval by Woodrow Wilson, this maxim has a doubtful moral history. He used it against our enemies in the First World War to dismember the Austro-Hungarian and Ottoman Empires, with results which hardly inspire enthusiasm today. After the Second World War the doctrine was invoked against our friends in the dissolution of their colonial connections. In all probability these connections would inevitably have been dissolved. But the results were immeasurably improved when considerations other than moralistic maxims were brought to bear on the process.

# Ethics in International Relations Today

On the one occasion when the right of self-determination—then called secession—was invoked against our own government by the Confederate States of America, it was rejected with a good deal of bloodshed and moral fervor. Probably you agree that it was rightly rejected. You would doubtless also agree that the dialogue now in progress between the British- and French-speaking sections of Canada upon the problems of a common national life together would not be helped by conducting it in terms of the principle of self-determination.

Furthermore, this moralistic doctrine is not merely no help to wise policy decisions, it can be a positive menace to them. "Hitler's appeal to national self-determination in the Sudeten crisis in 1938," writes Henry Kissinger, "was an invocation of 'justice,' and thereby contributed to the indecisiveness of the resistance; it induced the Western powers to attempt to construct a 'truly' legitimate order by satisfying Germany's 'just' claims. Only after Hitler annexed Bohemia and Moravia was it clear that he was aiming for dominion, not legitimacy; only then did the contest become one of pure power."

Another set of moralisms and maxims crops up to bedevil discussion and decision about what is broadly called "foreign aid." A good deal of trouble comes from the anthropomorphic urge to regard nations as individuals and apply to our own national conduct vague maxims for individual conduct—for instance, the Golden Rule—even though in practice individuals rarely practice it. The fact is that nations are not

133

individuals; the cause and effect of their actions are wholly different; and what a government can and should do with the resources which it takes from its citizens must be governed by wholly different considerations from those which properly determine an individual's use of his own.

This does not mean that considerations of compassion have no place in governmental decisions. It does mean that the criteria are generally quite different and far more complicated. Some of these criteria will determine what funds can be made available; others will determine their allocation among uses always exceeding amounts available.

The overriding guide must be achievement of a major goal of policy—in this case, creating an environment in which free societies may flourish and undeveloped nations who want to work on their own development may find the means to do so. This is an exceedingly difficult matter for both aiding and aided governments. The criteria should be hard-headed in the extreme. Decisions are not helped by considering them in terms of sharing, brotherly love, the Golden Rule, or inducting our citizens into the Kingdom of Heaven.

But, you will say to me, at least one moral standard of right and wrong has been pretty well agreed to be applicable to foreign policy. Surely, the opinion of the world has condemned the use and threat of force by one state against another, as the United Nations Charter bears witness. Does this not give us firm ground on which to stand? Well, does it? Ever since the Charter was signed, those whose interests are opposed to ours have used force, or the threat of it, whenever it seemed to them advisable and safe—in Greece, Czechoslovakia, Palestine, Berlin, Korea, Indochina, and Hungary. Each side used it in regard to Suez.

Is it moral to deny ourselves the use of force in all circumstances, when our adversaries employ it, under handy excuses, whenever it seems useful to tip the scales of power against every value we think of as moral and as making life worth living? It seems to me not only a bad bargain, but a stupid one. I would almost say an immoral one. For the very conception of morality seems to me to involve a duty to preserve values outside the contour of our own skins, and at the expense of foregoing much that is desired and pleasant, including—it may be—our own fortunes and lives.

But, however that may be, those involved in the Cuban crisis of October 1962 will remember the irrelevance of the supposed moral considerations brought out in the discussions. Judgment centered about the appraisal of dangers and risks, the weighing of the need for decisive and effective action against considerations of prudence; the need to do enough, against the consequences of doing too much. Moral talk did not bear on the problem. Nor did it bear upon the decision of those called upon to advise the President in 1949 whether and with what degree of urgency to press the attempt to produce a thermonuclear weapon. A respected colleague advised me that it would be better that our whole nation and people should perish rather than be party to a course so evil as producing that weapon. I told him that on the Day of Judgment his view might be confirmed and that he was free to go forth and preach the necessity for salvation. It was not, however, a view which I could entertain as a public servant.

What, then, is the sound approach to questions of foreign policy? I suggest that it is what we might call the strategic approach—to consider various courses of action from the point of view of their bearing upon major objectives. On August 22, 1862, President Lincoln wrote Horace Greeley in response to the latter's question as to how the President viewed the question of slavery in relation to the war then in progress,

> my paramount object in this struggle is to save the Union, and is not either to save or destroy slavery. If I could save the Union without freeing any slave, I would do it; and if I could save it by freeing some and leaving others alone, I would also do that. What I do about slavery and the colored race, I do because I believe it helps to save this Union; and what I forbear, I forbear because I do not believe it would help to save the Union. I shall do less whenever I shall believe what I am doing hurts the cause, and I shall do more whenever I shall believe doing more will help the cause.

This is what I mean by the strategic approach. If you object that it is no different from saying that the end justifies the means, I must answer that in foreign affairs only the end can justify the means; that this is not to say that the end justifies any means, or that some ends can justify anything. The shifting *combina-*

*zioni,* sought by the weak Italian city states of the Renaissance to plunder one another, not only failed to justify the means they used, but gave their diplomacy and its expounder, Niccolò Machiavelli, the bad name they have today.

The end sought by our foreign policy, the purpose for which we carry on relations with foreign states, is, as I have said, to preserve and foster an environment in which free societies may exist and flourish. Our policies and actions must be tested by whether they contribute to or detract from achievement of this end. They need no other justification or moral or ethical embellishment. To oppose powerful and brutal states which threaten the independence of others is not less admirable because it helps secure our own as well; nor is it less good to help others improve their lot because it is necessary to keep the free world free and to strengthen it.

In conducting our foreign affairs we can use any amount of intelligence, perseverance, nerve, and luck. But if we have an excess of moral or ethical enthusiasm or idealism, let us not try to find an outlet for it in the formulation of foreign policies. Rather in how we carry them out. In this country we have an unfortunate tendency to do fine and noble things in a thoroughly churlish way. Let us remember that often what we do may be less important than how we do it. "What one lives for may be uncertain," writes Lord David Cecil. "How one lives is not." We can be faulted far less in what we do than in how we do it.

# *Ambivalences of American Foreign Policy*

Critics of American foreign policy since the Second World War have thought they found in it an ambivalence: a pentecostal gift of tongues urging at the same time our revelation of the Celestial City on earth, the abode of Peace, Progress, the Brotherhood of Man; and, contrarily, the necessity of spending more than half our governmental budget through the Pentagon, the Atomic Energy Commission, and the Central Intelligence Agency. The critics have been quite right; and would have been more charitable had they seen the explanation in history rather than in hypocrisy. For we inherited the revelation and our faith in it from nineteenth-century Britain, our immediate political ancestor. Our more mundane preoccupations were forced upon us by the times in which we live.

Address delivered at the University of Indiana, March 5, 1965.

# Ambivalences of American Foreign Policy

The nineteenth century, although unique in human history, paradoxically has given us our ideal of normality. It stands alone and apart amid millennia in which man's struggle to survive and multiply hardly kept him ahead of extinction by pestilence and disaster, when war was the common lot far more often than peace, and when all that each pitifully short generation could pass on to the next was barely enough to support a meager life.

Never, before the nineteenth century, had man so escaped the curse of war. Only two centuries earlier one-third of Europe's people had perished in the thirty years of war over religion; and Napoleon had run up a formidable total in the wars just ended. Never, since the discovery of wheel and sail, had economic advance been so great. Never had people, goods, and ideas moved so freely over the globe; perhaps, never to move so freely again. Truly, out of all history, here was the century of progress, of unparalleled growth of capital and population, and, as Lord Acton saw it, of liberty as well.

To those in the nineteenth century who shaped our American intellectual inheritance, to the English romantics, the perfectability of man seemed assured; the Kingdom of Heaven on earth, just around the corner. Europe was skeptical. There the Prophets of Progress had had their day and departed. Africa remained a dark continent; Asia, except for India, a closed one; and Latin America, exhausted by Spanish spoliation, lay somnolent and apart under the Monroe Doctrine. But in England, amid the misery of the industrial revolution, eager spirits caught the flush of a dawn which was to be the millennium. Tennyson in *Locksley Hall* identified the vision explicitly for his contemporaries.

. . . the war-drum throbb'd no longer, and the battle-flags were furl'd
In the Parliament of man, the Federation of the world.

There the common sense of most shall hold a fretful realm in awe,
And the kindly earth shall slumber, lapt in universal law.

The date was 1842. If forty years later the vision had faded for his Lordship, it still appeared brightly to his American disciples across the ocean. By the end of the century the American army and navy had become largely of ceremonial utility—as the Spanish War warned us—and American diplomacy became obsessed in the next decade with the negotiation of a long series of unused treaties of arbitration. The Permanent Court of Arbitration was established in 1907, and 1913 saw the completion of Mr. Carnegie's Peace Palace to house it in the Hague just in time for the First World War. For four years the two pinnacles of nineteenth-century political idealism—the judicial settlement of international disputes and the conception of a league to enforce peace—seemed to have been swept away.

But this view overlooked the powerful personality and convictions of a man who was both at the center of power and the embodiment of the nineteenth-century evangelical intellectual. Woodrow Wilson's intellectual life was spanned by Appomatox and Sarajevo, and the early part of it spent south of the Mason-Dixon line. His mind took form in the atmosphere of a Presbyterian manse and of Virginia, Johns Hopkins, and Princeton universities. His vision of man's future on earth was that of *Locksley Hall*. In the Senate battle over the League of Nations the victim of Messrs. Lodge and Johnson was not the vision of a world "lapt in universal law," but "an old man broken with the storms of state." The vision lived on. So deep and persistent a part of the American psyche was it that years later Calvin Coolidge sought to propitiate it by offering the Kellogg-Briand Pact to outlaw war, a path to salvation without priesthood or organization of any sort, the very epitome of salvation by faith.

The vision outlived Franklin Roosevelt's early period of isolationism and Senator Nye's later neutrality. Finally, when the Second World War burst upon a country unbelieving and aghast, so strong were the gospel and memory of the crucified Wilson that the country was seized with a sense of national sin. Mr. Cordell Hull, a fundamentalist in foreign affairs, did not shrink from the view that World War II was the price exacted by a relentless God for the repudiation of the Covenant of the League, and, like Lincoln referring to the cause of another war, was prepared to agree that "the judgments of the Lord are true and righteous altogether."

An aging Moses, Mr. Hull presided vaguely over the preparations for the journey to the Promised Land he was not to enter. Sweeping generalization—which Lincoln called "pernicious abstraction"—was more congenial to Mr. Hull than concentration upon the location and movement of power, its likely use, and pressures which could affect the actions of states, beneficially or otherwise. He was fascinated too by another conception of *Locksley Hall,* the application to international relations of analogies to the political structure of democratic states. This preoccupation with "machinery," as we call organization, has special attraction for Americans.

President Roosevelt, and after him President Truman, were converted to the faith that the first order of business after victory should be the creation of the United Nations to be the guardian of peace, the votary of law under the Charter, and the instrument of material progress. Mr. Churchill rejected conversion and remained obstinately concentrated upon Soviet exercises of power in Eastern and Central Europe. The Aaron who guided the entrance to the Promised Land of World Organization was Edward R. Stettinius, Secretary of State from November 1944 to July 1945. His forte was rather energetic attention to detail in operations selected by others than comprehension of events seen as a whole. By the time he had completed his work, seen it ratified by the participating nations, and its institutions and habitat established, the attention of those in charge of American foreign policy was urgently commanded elsewhere.

What so urgently commanded their attention was the collapse of the world order of the nineteenth century, the structure which gave verisimilitude to its conception of One World moved by inevitable progress to Federation under a Parliament of man. This structure, brilliantly fashioned by Castlereagh and Metternich after the Republican and Napoleonic wars, rested on the concert of the great empires of Europe and their colonial systems. Under it, throughout the world, the ambitious were restrained, the disorderly suppressed by force, and all played roles in a world-wide economy to which impersonal forces had assigned them. This system, the only true world order which has ever existed, was self-destroyed by what Desmond Donnelly has called the European Civil War of 1914 to 1945.

The principle which had gained acceptance for the concert within Europe was the right of legitimate governments to exist. The sanction was the organization of power against a disturber of its arranged balance. Its weakness lay in the unobserved movement eastward of the center of power in Europe. As late as the second decade of the nineteenth century, twenty years of war and the follies of Napoleon, which so exasperated Talleyrand, barely enabled all the rest of Europe to contain the power of France. A century later the added power of the United States was twice needed to prevent German hegemony. When German power had been destroyed, the center of power again moved eastward to the Soviet Union. How this power would be used, and what combination of strength and will could restrain it was not immediately discernible.

The old One World order had been destroyed utterly and forever. Even its foundations, the great empires of Europe and their colonial possessions, like those of Carthage, had been plowed and sown with salt by the thirty years of civil war in Europe. The state of affairs, the facts of international life, which underlay the assumptions of the nineteenth century had gone.

Not all of this was immediately clear as the smoke of battle rolled away. The destruction in Europe and in the Far East was plain enough; but its implications there and elsewhere were not. It took time to see the extent to which power had been destroyed and bonds had been loosed, how deeply—even within established societies—authority and mutual trust had been undermined, the very conceptions of legitimacy had decayed, and the political postulates of the time had become those of a revolutionary age. To penetrate the obscurity from which these somber realities were emerging and anticipate their impact upon the external world and our own position in it became the daily business of our foreign office.

By its very nature it was an empirical business. Quickly discernible was the immediate predicament of our friends and allies in Europe. In moving swiftly to meet this, we learned much and fast. We learned that our former ally, the Soviet Union, was determined to divide Europe in the middle by a north-south line and to drop an "iron curtain," in Mr. Churchill's phrase, upon the eastern half, that it placed first priority on the development of its own military power, including nuclear armament, that its attitude toward the United States was one of intense suspicion and hostility; and that, while probing with instruments of subversion and military power for weak spots beyond its controlled area, it would allow no interference within by international agencies or otherwise.

From 1946 to 1949 the Government of the United States tried to solve the unsettled problems left over from the war by negotiation with the Soviet Union, both through the United Nations and bilaterally. The result was total negation and failure, whether the problem was the international control of atomic energy, the economic reconstruction of Europe, the issues of Berlin and the unification of Germany, the future of the Eastern Mediterranean, especially Greece and Turkey, the unification of Korea, or a peace treaty with Japan. Convinced by these experiences that the Soviet Union was not prepared to negotiate tolerable solutions of these problems in the then state of affairs, the American government came to a basic decision and began to act upon it. The decision was that the world of the last half of the twentieth century was, and would continue to be, a divided world. The action was to make the free—that is, the non–Communist-dominated—part of that divided world as secure and flourishing as possible and to establish a sound basis of acceptability—or, if one likes, of legitimacy—for it. By this last we mean a foundation of principle and practice which would gain acceptance in a broad enough area to provide spaciousness for free societies.

To take this decision and action while proclaiming stoutly the faith of our fathers' as stated in the United

Nations Charter and embodied in its Organization was bound to produce dilemmas and ambivalences. For we could hardly act simultaneously on the premises that the world was united for peace and brotherhood and divided by fear and irreconcilable purposes without producing inconsistency in our professions and, even worse, confusion among us about the right course to follow and, hence, as to the right day-to-day decisions.

Our education was quick and expensive; but not so expensive as it might have been. To begin with, we had to learn how wrong the prophets of the Enlightenment had been about what moved peoples. They overestimated the influence of wisdom, virtue, and understanding of experience and underestimated prejudice, passion, and dogma. They rated too highly gratitude, sentiment, even what they called "enlightened self-interest"; and were unaware of the power of nationalism and xenophobia when aroused by a Peron, Nasser, Sukarno, or even anonymous manipulators of "students." We learned for ourselves what Oxenstierna, Gustavus Adolphus's Chancellor, taught his son always to remember—"with how little wisdom the world is governed."

Then there was power. We had been brought to think of power as the instrument of corruption. Lord Acton, again, was our authority for that. Power politics had no place in our Celestial City, but a substantial place in the twentieth century. We learned in a rough school the importance of power, its natures, and its limitations. Two wars, and our behavior be-

tween them, made clear its importance. Its composition
we learned from having to produce it again after 1940.
The formula calls for population, resources, technology, and will. Napoleon rated the importance of the
last element to all the others at a ratio of three to one.
His successor, General de Gaulle, by substituting will
for all the others, seeks to create an illusion of power.
The rest of Europe, lacking will, pretends, without
much conviction, that economic prosperity alone con-
stitutes power. But both are wrong. Will, by fusing
and using the other elements to a purpose, gives a
society its impact upon its contemporaries.

We learned that military power is primarily effective against opposing military power and, by over-
awing and overcoming it, enhances acceptance of its
possessor's will and purposes. But physical force soon
runs into limitations in imposing acceptance on minds
not wholly governed by reason or fear of physical suffering. Even the Inquisition required more favorable
circumstances and a longer time for coercion than are
apt to be available today. So when people say that
our soldiers win wars only to have our diplomats lose
the peace, the truths which puzzle them are that military force is not so potent as they had thought, and
people are more intractable.

We had just finished this high school stage in our
education when we were called upon to take the lead
in a task in some ways more formidable than the one
described in the first chapter of Genesis. The problem
there was to create a world out of chaos; ours, to create
half a world out of the same material without blowing

the whole thing apart in the process. Like Archimedes, we had first to find a place to stand and collaborators in the effort. Both were found in Europe, and both had to be restored, before the work began. Our purpose this evening is not to retell how Europe was reborn and the European–North American nucleus of the free half-world formed, but to trace the origins and point out the consequences of the ambivalences in our policies.

As already suggested, it was soon brought home to us that our interests and purposes and those of the Soviets, in Europe to begin with, were quite antithetical. Four-power occupation of Germany quickly turned into the confrontation known as the "blockade of Berlin." From then on, the movement was swift, from the efforts of 1948 to deal with Europe within the concepts and methods of the United Nations—the idea that builders and wreckers could work together happily and simultaneously toward a common end— to a direct showdown of purpose and power. When, as a result, negotiation had been restricted to those who had a common purpose, action began.

In an amazingly short time, will toward a common end had been organized and backed by vast resources and imaginative methods of economic, military, and political action. The Marshall Plan, NATO, the bringing of our former enemies into close alliance, changed the whole structure and balance of international relations. New problems of trans-Atlantic relations have been produced in plenty; but they are the problems of convalescence to vigorous health, not those of illness. Europe, or part of it, has mistaken prosperity and a stubborn pride for power. Despite the difficulties which the latter creates, it is far better to have some of the elements of power than none of them. With patience these difficulties can be surmounted provided our European allies, or most of them, will act together with us on immediate practical problems in the conviction that they are common problems and require common solutions. These immediate tasks are the multilateral force and NATO military policy for the next decade, the Kennedy round of trade negotiations, a common and sensible agricultural policy, and a modernization (for the next twenty years) of international monetary arrangements. The arrangements made twenty years ago at Bretton Woods, and the economic policies of expanding production and trade for which they were designed, have been so incredibly successful that the facilities need to be enlarged again.

The negotiations essential here are between a small group, not exclusively with our European allies because monetary affairs particularly require Switzerland and Japan. The interests of others are vitally involved, too, and must be dealt with fairly, but not by the kleig-light, loudspeaker methods of a political convention. What is required is open covenants, secretly arrived at, drafted by indispensable parties (those without whose adherence agreements will not work). Agreements on tariffs, for instance, where the widest acceptance should be an aim, can be made so by those who look outward with the realization that expansion is the essence of economic growth and that expansion cannot long be maintained by inward-looking, parochial policies.

The past summer opened broad opportunity for the display of ambivalence. In the military field we proposed the multilateral force, designed to give our allies a practical means of participating in the responsibility for and operation of nuclear weapons without the fateful step of separate national forces. The step at once met the opposition of the French and British governments, both of which—in addition to possible broader aims—had the advantage of appearing more nuclear-powered than the Germans. At the same time, it aroused cries of duplicity in the United Nations for undercutting our professed aim of preventing the diffusion of nuclear weapons. Protests that diffusion was exactly what we had been trying to prevent were lost in the clamor of Russian propaganda.

Then, too, at Geneva, discussing international trade agreements in private with the Common Market countries, and in the United Nations forum with the undeveloped ones, we stood firmly, first, for freer trade than the former wanted and, then, for not so free trade as the undeveloped countries demanded but were not willing to give. So to the despair of our speech writers and formula seekers we alternately pushed forward and held back.

But the undeveloped countries have always put this strain on our rhetoric. According to deep-seated and related American principles, disapproval of colonialism, and belief in President Wilson's right to national self-determination, their birth should have been indeed a blessed event to be welcomed joyously. But we became a professional midwife not for joy in the work, or belief that offspring were ready or mothers reconciled to parturition, but because, if long delayed in the mothers' weakened condition the result could well be fatal. In Indochina, the East Indies, the Indian sub-continent, the Near East, and Africa, it happened over and over again. The mere thought of the United States became repulsive to prospective mothers, and for some time after the event.

The consequences of the population explosion did not, of course, stop here. First of all the expense of child care became in large part transferred from parent to midwife, either directly or through the international orphan asylum, the United Nations. The burden, though heavy, was shouldered as an obligation of responsible leadership. Recently, however, the conviction has grown that the orphanage was being run by the infants and some of the older children whose development had been retarded. This has brought second thoughts.

The young reach physical maturity fast in warm climates. Soon the new nations were in long pants, and the starting membership of the United Nations had more than doubled. The expenses of the new nations had grown, too. Embassies, armies, revolutions, dictators—especially dictators, like Sukarno, who distract attention from failures at home by expansion abroad—are expensive.

Then there was development. It is proper and right that young nations should develop, and a responsibility of their elders in any acceptable half-world system that this should be possible. But, as we are learning at home as well as abroad, they can do so only by acquiring first sound bodies, the three R's of education, and the acceptance of discipline. Such was the doctrine stated in Point Four of President Truman's inaugural address on January 20, 1949.

The way to develop is to improve agriculture, build schools and train teachers for elementary and some secondary and technical education, and to control population. What most countries too frequently demand are a steel mill, an airline, protective tariff, and the nationalization of whatever exists already. The belief seems to exist, too, that independence should itself bring industrial maturity, since colonialism, capitalism, or some other malfeasance of the developed countries has been responsible for economic backwardness. This is called the revolution of rising expectations. An earnest desire to help others has been interpreted as a confession of guilt; a hesitation to meet large demands has been answered by the threat to go Communist.

At best the relations between the developing and the developed states, between the aided and the aiding, are difficult. The difficulty does not raise doubt that it is more blessed to give than to receive, but rather whether accepted notions in the United Nations are, after all, sensible and whether they may not bear some responsibility for the state of international juvenile delinquency today.

The Charter, like the by-laws of a club, omits the

# Ambivalences of American Foreign Policy

more important rules of conduct, taking them as understood. There are no rules against interrupting talk by beating on desks with one's shoes, destroying the furniture, stealing other members' coats and hats, or committing assault and battery on the premises. But this economy of words has not worked well in the United Nations. Most members read the Charter as laying down only one rule and this rule they interpret in an interesting way. The rule is that force or the threat of force may not be used against any member state. According to the Soviet Union, the rule does not read against what it refers to as "wars of national liberation," nor to force used at the request of a Communist government to suppress uprisings of its own people. But it does apply according to Messrs. Sukarno, Nasser, and Nkrumah against aid given by whites to a Negro government attempting to put down rebellion fomented and supplied by Communist or other Negro governments.

While the Charter refers approvingly to justice and more sparingly to law, no content of either is provided. But the Charter's goals are made clear. They are peace, sometimes described as peace with justice, and economic development. The obligation of all members is to further both. The number of members who have the capacity and desire to do much outside their borders about either—to say nothing of both— is very small indeed. The number who are entitled to take part in laying down proposed plans and policies is very large. The doctrines of universality of membership and sovereign equality of state have seen to that.

It can be seen, now, why the relations between the developed and the developing nations are bound to be difficult. The great economic development of the nineteenth century was financed by the money centers of Europe, organized into a single economy through colonial empires, operated under legal principles giving security to investment, and policed by force. It produced phenomenal development. One of its prize exhibits was the United States. The outflow of capital from Europe for foreign investment was immense. "If the same proportion of American resources were devoted to foreign investment as Britain devoted . . . in 1913, the flow of investment would require to be thirty times as large. The entire Marshall Plan would have to be carried out twice a year." [1]

All of this ended with the European Civil War. We would not wish it back if we could have our wish granted. Although the system worked wonders, it also worked harshly, and with the same disregard for its human tools abroad as was shown at home. But human exploitation is no more inherent in foreign investment than in investment at home. What is essential is order, mutuality of obligation, and respect for contracts. The international development system of the nineteenth century is dead. It has been succeeded by something approaching international anarchy, with a non-legal system providing safe haven for expropriators and defaulting debtors, and an ethos favoring the rejection of discipline, control, and restraint of any kind. Mr.

1. A. K. Cairncross, *Home and Foreign Investment 1870–1913* (London: Cambridge University Press, 1953), p. 3.

# Ambivalences of American Foreign Policy

Nasser was performing true to this ethos when in the same week he permitted the burning of our government information library, in protest against our help to the Belgians and Mr. Tshombe in rescuing white missionaries in the Congo, and demanded more American wheat to feed his people.

The serpent of the old Nile seems to bring out the worst of our ambivalent performances. The worst was certainly Suez, where the word is quite inadequate for a recent American critic who charges our policy with downright and deliberate deceit. It is more charitable to attribute it to a schizothymia brought on by inability to reconcile the ideational content of our professions with the practical needs of action in contemporary life.

Ambivalence in our foreign policy and practice of diplomacy will continue until our minds escape from the nineteenth century and the dead hand of a vanished world. A good way to begin our escape is to de-romanticize the United Nations, to see it not as "the town meeting of the world" or as the "last best hope of earth," but as Dag Hammarskjold saw it. In his fourth annual report as Secretary General he warns us that it is not world government in embryo, but an additional means to be used by those who wish to resolve differences and find solutions.

But if it is accepted that the primary value of the United Nations is to serve as an instrument for negotiation among governments and for concerting action by governments in support of the goals of the Charter, it is also necessary, I believe, to use the legislative procedures of the United Nations consistently in ways which will promote these ends. In an organization of sovereign states, voting victories are likely to be illusory unless they are steps in the direction of winning lasting consent to a peaceful and just settlement of the question at issue.

This, as the Book of Common Prayer puts it, is a "true saying and worthy of all men to be received."

For those who conceive of negotiations as war by another means, a method of dividing allies and isolating and weakening an enemy, the United Nations becomes no more than another battlefield in the cold war. To this we should add that it is not how we in this country regard the United Nations that counts. Indeed, a good deal of our confusion comes from the fact that we regard it one way while others have been regarding it quite differently and using it for quite opposed purposes.

The ambivalence in our foreign policy does not come from swings between idealism and Machiavellianism, but between sleepwalking in a dream and alertness in a daylight world. What this country has achieved in the last twenty years on the world scene has been so far beyond expectation and belief that we need not despair of the future. We shall do well to keep our wits and perceptions sharp and employ our native instinct for orderly work.

# The Call of Duty

You have honored me greatly this evening by the warmth of your reception of a warrior long since retired from the fray, by the munificence and generosity of your award, and by the kindness that you have lavished upon my wife and myself. May I confess that I find myself in ageement with some of the dissidents from this evening's program who thought the honor beyond my deserts. They are quite right —which makes me all the more appreciative of it. Perhaps the very essence of feeling honored is the knowledge that the accolade is undeserved. One must be assured indeed, to believe that one has ever acted above and beyond what was reasonably to be expected of one—in other words, the call of duty. For while

Address given at the inauguration of the *Milwaukee Journal*–World Affairs Council of Milwaukee Annual Award for Distinguished Service in Foreign Affairs, October 10, 1969.

many may exaggerate the value of their contribution, few can honestly exaggerate the call of duty. I am grateful and deeply touched that you should have inaugurated this award by selecting me as its first recipient.

In discussion with so cosmopolitan an audience as this, which has blood and cultural ties all over the world, it is natural that one's thoughts should turn to that "vast external realm," as the Supreme Court has described the world beyond our borders, and to our relations with it. Just having finished a book on our foreign relations over a good part of my life, which is published this very day, I shall not now look backward at the past. Instead we might peer together into the future, not to attempt to predict it—a form of hubris that invites rebuke from the gods—but to see whether presently visible trends and conditions throw light on the nature of problems that may arise and the quality of governments throughout the world which will have to deal with them. Knowing this much should help us toward some notions of what to expect.

Starting at home, what sort of mood possesses us and is likely to continue for some time? Certainly not the buoyant courage that led the country to meet the near panic brought by the depression with the belief that all we had to fear was fear itself. Not the grim determination that met the attack at Pearl Harbor and smashed enemies on both sides of the world bent on our destruction. Not the mood of vigorous and inspired leadership that brought restoration to war-torn countries, help and guidance to new ones, and protection to the free portion of the world from the aggression of a new ideologically inspired imperialism.

No; today the mood is not one of buoyancy in the face of challenge but of disillusionment that the labor "naught availeth," and weariness of well-doing and leadership. This is not because the tasks of leadership are beyond the capacity and strength of this country, but because some tasks chosen were ill-chosen, because all are difficult, and because thinking about them makes us tired. Nevertheless, the mood is real and will continue until changed by time, luck, and a new gift of strong leadership.

At home our problems in a way come from success, not failure. In the past forty years the material welfare of all sections of our people and the justice and humanity with which the needs and condition of the weak and heavy-laden have been met have exceeded all promise of our preceding history. Yet, domestic tranquility, one of the principal purposes of organized society, has rarely been more disturbed. This disturbance comes from the impact of various minority groups upon the rest of us—the black minority protesting with violence against discriminations; the adolescent-juvenile minority protesting against the war in Vietnam and also against things as they are, as rising generations have done with varying degrees of trouble for their elders since the beginning of recorded history; the criminal minority in its historic effort to redistribute property; and so on.

These troubles, painful as they are, should not surprise us. The first two have historically accompanied periods of social improvement, not those of social stagnation and depression. Explanation of the third was given by my son when, as District Attorney, he was asked by a congressional committee to what he attributed the growth of crime in our district. "To people," he answered, "and especially to large and sudden increases of them."

Our present domestic discontents and, hence, the domestic problems of government, stem from three sources—the Vietnam war, internal disorder, and the inflation caused by the expense of these troubles plus that of national defense. The rest are subsidiary. Problems are difficult but not impossible to solve. Indeed, the chief difficulty comes not from determining what to do, but from summoning the resolution to do it and rallying support for the attempt.

For instance, internal disorder has long-term causes and cures about which innumerable commissions have written interminably. It also has immediate and painful impacts that call for immediate and strong preventive measures. An end to long-term causes of disorder may well require a solution in Vietnam, more and better education, and the end of poverty and racial discrimination; but a government that tolerates disorder until these goals are achieved will not survive. Disorder can be drastically reduced before its causes are altogether removed. To do so will require federal initiative and cooperation with local authorities.

Disorder, whether from extensive rioting our individual crimes of violence, will not occur in the presence of alert and overwhelming power. The Congress can direct the President when domestic tranquility is threatened by violence national in scope and nature, such as race rioting, to send Federal armed forces into a threatened community to support local forces, without waiting for invitation or violence. These forces should be instructed to make their presence known and be prepared to preserve order and protect persons and property whenever preventive or corrective action might be necessary. Among the purposes for which "We the people of the United States . . . [did] . . . ordain and establish this Constitution for the United States of America" was to "insure domestic tranquility." Only force in being and in timely position can insure domestic tranquility against the dangers that have harassed us for too long and are still harassing us.

Similarly, to bring us relief from crime on the streets, which in my own community makes it hazardous to mail a letter or walk a dog after dark, a well-tested method is at hand in Federal aid in the financing and training of considerable increments to local police forces. The best insurance of safety on the street is more policemen patrolling them. A great deal of heat can be generated in debating the treatment of persons apprehended for crime during and after their arrest, trial, and conviction. Everything that makes for virtue is desirable, but clearly the way to bring about the largest and fastest reduction in crime is to reduce the opportunity to commit it. To do that we need more and better policemen. As already stated, the difficulty in stopping internal disorder, as in dealing with other domestic problems, is not in knowing what to do, but in getting on with it.

Why is it harder for governments to act than to know how to act? Because, I suggest, all governments in power today everywhere in the world are weak governments. Sometimes because they are made up of weak or inexperienced men; sometimes because their support in the society is weak. The latter is the source of our own government's weakness. It was a minority government when elected and has not been able to forge adequate new support. Consequently, it has been hesitant, indecisive, over-responsive to criticism from country and Congress. Perhaps the United States Senate would do well to ponder the proposition that the separation of powers, like matrimony, presupposes a nice balance between mutual support and mutual criticism. If the latter too greatly overbalances the former, the result is likely to be disastrous to the union. Broadly, the President has shown good initial judgment. All of us should do all we can to help him and nothing to make his road harder. I have been doing so and will keep on doing so. Too many believe that to warrant support a President should deserve it by being one of those rare leaders who dominate and determine the nature of their times as Charlemagne did his, or as the great Elizabeth did hers, or as FDR did in our own time. Try as you will, you cannot find in this continent, South America, or Europe or Asia or Africa—in the free world or in the Communist—a better than average government, black, white, or yellow. Those who have been eager for the century of the common man should be happy, for we are now certainly well into one.

What does it mean for us all, this rule everywhere by median men? What sort of problems will it raise? What sort of responses will be made to them? Almost everywhere the cause and effect of change will not be understood, for both will be complex; hence change will be regarded with apprehension, if not with fear. But responses will differ. In authoritarian regimes an almost reflexive reaction may try to repress change, as the Communist alliance is attempting to do in Czechoslovakia; in liberal democracies, to appease it, as some liberal religious organizations are attempting to appease black nationalist demands for reparations. Both repression and appeasement are traditional, almost instinctive responses to fear. "Nice doggie!" we say to the vicious mongrel growling at our heels; or, if we dare, fetch him a clout with a walking stick. Neither is likely to be the result of careful thought.

Turning from general to more specific considerations, what we may expect from both enemies and friends seems unlikely to make for stability and easier relations. The Soviet Government over the past decade has doubled its expenditures for strategic nuclear power, developing a military force second to none. At the same time our own expenditure on these weapons has been reduced by half. We are approaching, if we have not reached, a parity. To the chronically hopeful among us this suggests an approach also to easier relations between us, a period of *détente* in which discussion might lead to a reduction or end to rival arming.

# This Vast External Realm

They hail Foreign Minister Gromyko's statement that "the Soviet Union has always proceeded on the assumption that the U.S.S.R. and the U.S.A. can find a common language" and wanted good and friendly relations. The first half of the statement was false historically; the second half was negatived at the same international Communist meeting at the Kremlin in June by Gromyko's and the Communist Party's boss, Mr. Brezhnev. "The United States of America," he said, "the chief imperialist power, has grown more aggressive. . . . Global in scale, the basic contradiction between imperialism and socialism is growing deeper . . . the struggle between the two world systems is becoming sharper. . . ."

Nevertheless, according to Party doctrine, the great growth of Soviet military power had prevented an attack by the United States in an effort to preserve the imperialist system. Soviet power had also made possible prevention of defections from its own system— i.e., Czechoslovakia—and the support of wars of national liberation against "capitalist imperialism." Both forms of military action are wholly consistent with "peaceful coexistence" since they are forms of self-defense against counter-revolutionary reaction. For those interested in Communist logic—dialectical materialism—the Gromyko and Brezhnev statements are quite reconcilable and both Soviet aid to the Viet Minh and the attempt to place nuclear missiles in Cuba were in pursuit of good and friendly relations with the United States through peaceful coexistence.

However, for those more interested in Soviet conduct than in verbal agility, the forthcoming nuclear arms limitation talks offer a more promising field for speculation. One can easily see the advantage to the Soviet Union and the lethal danger to the United States in an agreement that would bind the open and public American society to nuclear parity with the Soviet Union without opening the closed and secret Soviet society to far more inspection and oversight than it has ever been willing to grant in twenty years of discussion of the subject. The chances of success in these discussions stated numerically must be almost infinitesimal, yet the lure of them to negotiators and the danger of falling into their own bear trap is substantial. Until Communist society becomes more civilized and reliable, the risks of improvident agreement, like those of continuous Russian roulette, are uninsurable, and perhaps greater than those created by no agreement at all.

They seem even greater when we add another consideration. At present the Soviet Union greatly surpasses Western Europe in intermediate-range ballistic missiles and conventional forces. The threat that this superior power might impose Soviet demands on Western Europe, as it has on Eastern Europe, has been offset by the provisions of the North Atlantic Treaty and the presence in Europe of substantial United States conventional forces as a practical guarantee of U.S. strategic nuclear support. If, however, Soviet and American intercontinental nuclear power were neutralized by agreement to maintain parity leaving Soviet intermediate-range and conventional power unchallengeable, the balance of power in Europe would be so openly and notoriously upset that the imbalance might be as great and could be as decisive as it was after Munich. Not that war would be inevitable, but Soviet domination *would* be if American intervention should be foreclosed.

One does not need to suppose a Soviet attack on Western Europe to bring this result about. More likely, growing tension in Eastern Europe and Soviet demands upon Germany, like those of Hitler upon Czechoslovakia, would find weak and plausible politicians to grant them in the name of maintaining "peace in our time."

The way to this result could well be paved by the consequences within the Western alliance of weak governments there. Leadership is needed not only to move people forward but to restrain them. The common tendency is to follow short-range, narrowly conceived interests. That is why we pollute our environment, not only physical environment but political as well. The long-range interests of the Western world require increasing unity within Europe and between Europe and North America. To accomplish this requires strong leadership to control nationalist interests making for disunity and mutual irritation. Weak governments yield to centrifugal forces. These we see operating today. General de Gaulle's *folie de grandeur* and German pride in the strength of the mark prevented monetary adjustments in Europe until the forced devaluation of the franc precipitated a suspension of the unified agricultural policy in Europe and necessitated new trade restrictions. These can harm others, including the United States, and stimulate reciprocal protective measures.

Furthermore, de Gaulle's nationalist separatism weakened NATO, gave rise to irritated frustration with our allies, and led to the Mansfield-Symington proposal eighteen months ago for a withdrawal of American forces from Europe. From this folly we were saved by the Soviet invasion of Czechoslovakia. Saved may be too strong a word. More likely the agitation has only been postponed. One does not need a crystal ball to foresee how these actions and reactions, each popular and hard to resist in its own locality, could so loosen the bonds of the Atlantic Alliance as to open the way for Soviet prying into the cracks.

I am not predicting that these evils will come to pass or that signs portend the decline of the West. One cannot see so far; but far enough to warn of the direction of the wind and tide, to warn also that various ships of state lack experienced and wise captains in command, strong hands at the oars, and appointed destinations. Some appear to be on collision courses. The intervention of human will, ability, and courage could prevent disaster, but whence it will come is not shown by my crystal-gazing.

One can speak with more assurance of what to expect and what not to expect in our relations with the Southern hemisphere. There, on the whole, governments are weaker and less competent than elsewhere and our response to them is apt to be more doctrinaire and unwise. Government, as Plato taught, is an

art and the most difficult of all of them both to practice and to endure. Of all its forms democracy is the
most baffling and parliamentary democracy well-nigh
impossible. Even peoples of ancient culture such as
the French, Italians, and Greeks find it beyond them.
Yet this is the form that the European colonial powers
bequeathed to Africa and Asia, where it has largely
broken down. The same is generally true of that democratic obstacle race, known as the separation of powers,
which Latin America copied from the United States.

Lapses from the practice of these difficult procedures our press and public treat as falls from grace,
scolding the newer countries in sorrow but those who
should really know better, like the Greek colonels, in
anger. In doing so they forget what our founding fathers did not, that domestic tranquility is essential to
development of a new country. Only under conditions
of domestic order is capital formation possible. In
South America, Africa, and Asia the pressure of populations makes development a necessity. The cultural
blessings of civilization must await an equilibrium
between population and sustenance.

In some cases extreme zeal for democratic practices
unknown in our own country twenty years ago, such
as "one man—one vote," has led us to adopt hostile
attitudes towards countries in southern Africa which
are eager for good relations with us. In one instance,
that of Rhodesia, we have gone so far as to join in
economic warfare against her in the vain effort to
impose changes in her internal franchise laws. Here
our passion for democratic orthodoxy has overcome

our belief in material development, for the countries of southern Africa have developed economies more beneficial to their black as well as white citizens than any other in the continent. They can help the development of their black neighbor states—and are willing to do so—more than is possible for us. Moreover, their good will and the use of their ports is important to us as the Russian navy moves into the Indian Ocean.

So again in dealings with the southern hemisphere, as in our relations with the northern, we may expect to find weakness of governments leading to the triumph of unwise pressures and the neglect of common sense and national interests.

At present our relations with Peru furnish a lurid example. The military junta, seeking popularity, nationalized Standard of New Jersey's interest in a long-disputed oil concession. The United States Congress has imposed rigid restrictions on the President's freedom of negotiation in such cases. Nevertheless, with admirable restraint, the President has been seeking a solution, while Peru arrests fishing boats within two hundred miles of her coast.

All this may not be fatal but is unlikely to be beneficial.

Now that I am and have been for some time a private citizen, I am frequently asked what we citizens can do about these complex questions of our foreign relations. Here again the approach to the problem is simpler than the execution of it. As in every problem of private or business life, there is one fundamental primary rule: Try to understand the problem before devising an answer. Do this, and see how alone you are! Everyone—but everyone—knows answers, most of them conflicting. Politicians, commentators, and columnists are ready with answers to any question. Clergymen, professors, labor leaders, and students are overflowing with them. But if you go about like Diogenes with his lantern seeking, in this case, an understanding mind, you can discard most of the answers as no more meaningful than the shrill voices made by cicadas vibrating their abdominal membranes.

The facts are often hard to come by and open minds are rare. Fortunately, organizations exist to bring them together, of which the World Affairs Council movement stands in the forefront. Here the light of information and that of analysis are brought to bear upon problems. Time and again one discovers how often these converging lights show us the way, if not to the specific answer, at least to the area where an acceptable one may be found. To provide this enlightenment to citizens is a basic and invaluable part of the democratic process. That process consists of far more than counting heads. If they are not also filled and weighed, we hasten toward what Brooks Adams called the degradation of the democratic dogma.

I should also say to my inquiring fellow citizen that if knowledge and understanding of the problems is a sound way to begin private participation in foreign policy, opposition to government, for its own sake, is a poor way. We have inherited from colonial times a skepticism of government. The British were always restraining the colonists from lumbering masts—reserved for the royal navy—and from pushing into French and Indian territory. In our time, however, skepticism has progressed to instant opposition to any government proposal. To read and listen to public and private opinions would lead one to believe that we elect to public office the most zealous imbeciles bent upon every imaginable folly, extravagance, and disastrous adventure, determined to blight the hopes of the young, poor, and disadvantaged, and probably venal into the bargain. Even from the vantage-point of the opposition, this strikes me as an extreme view.

It is also a damaging and foolish one. The choices open to any responsible government here and now in dealing with the vast external realm are narrow ones. However much they may differ from our individual hopes and beliefs or from those of public pundits, they are not likely to be very different from what any person in public office might be able to do. Professional, even cantankerous, criticism is desirable to keep both the government and the governed alive to error and opportunity. However, as an attitude for the informed private citizen anxious to play a constructive role in policy-making, support of the responsible leader is a sound role.

As we noted earlier, his function in foreign policy is not only to lead in wise action but to restrain from foolish action. For both he needs support. Even a donkey responds to a carrot as well as a stick. In *Candide* Voltaire has an Englishman explain the execution of an English admiral on his own quarter-deck as an effort "pour encourager les autres." Indeed, to fall back on a more earthy saying of our own, it is a "hell of a way to run a railroad." Better ways are available right here in your own community. They require the hardest kind of work, which is thought. "The mode by which the inevitable comes to pass," it has been said, "is effort."

# Some Social Factors
# in Legal Change

As lawyers look about them today they see events which confuse and trouble them. A few years ago they saw an Iowa judge sitting in foreclosure cases. A group of mortgagors and their friends forcibly took him out of court, put a rope around his neck and made the gestures preliminary to a lynching. Foreclosures in that area stopped and action for the relief of debtors followed.

In Pennsylvania the lawyer sees unemployed miners mining and selling coal to which they have no legal title. The processes of law are powerless to enforce the rights of the legal owners. Recently in Michigan, the bar saw a judge, in accordance with traditional

Address given before the Law Club of Chicago, January 22, 1937.

173

principles of the law of property, order sit-down strikers to vacate a factory. The strikers refused to obey.
The force of the state was not employed to carry out
that order. Few informed persons thought that it would
be. These are only a few of the disturbing sights
which meet the lawyer's eye. They are not mentioned
as inclusive examples but to do what Meredith had
in mind when he spoke of "lapidary sentences which
perform the function of chalk eggs—they lure the sitter
to think."

What has brought about this divergence between
the law as it is written in the books and the law as it is
carried out? The press tells us that property rights are
yielding to human rights. This language only confuses
me. Men are not less concerned than formerly with
property. If anything, they are more concerned with
it. Property interests are not taking a position in the
background of human conflicts, which are the raw material of law.

What is happening, I believe, is that new interests
in property are pressing for recognition. But before
we can understand what is going on about us we must
free ourselves from the limitations of some concepts
which are very dear to lawyers, such concepts as
"ownership," "legal title," and "liberty of contract."
Tolstoy said: "One might explain to the dullest of
men the most difficult of problems, if he had no previous conception in regard to it, but it is impossible
to explain to the cleverest man even the simplest matters, if he is perfectly sure that he knows everything
about them." It would have been difficult to explain

these concepts which I have mentioned to a Western European six or seven hundred years ago. He would have been living in the age of feudalism to which our notion of "ownership" was wholly alien. What he understood was that people held property subject to the performance of certain duties.

Those duties had in the case of freemen very little economic character. They were directed toward carrying out the purposes of the system, military or political. Lower down in the system people held property on condition of performing labor on the estates of their superiors. But as between freemen, whether the property held was land or an office or a right to carry on a business, it was held, not under a condition of paying something which we would recognize as rent, not by rendering to the superior the economic equivalent, but by performing a duty which was designed to carry out the purposes of the system. These duties were, accepting the standards and purposes of the system, social obligations.

All through this system, from the very top to the very bottom, people were held together, not by rights, but by obligations. Often the burden of the obligation might outweigh the material benefits carried with it. Often it meant giving up one's life to carry out a duty designed to effectuate the ultimate purpose of the system. This purpose was security.

Then, too, this system was all-embracing. There were no people left out, no people who had no relation to property. Everybody, in some way or another, was attached to property—an attachment which gave

175

him the necessities of life and in turn required that he perform obligations necessary to the survival of the system.

You see at once how different all those conceptions are from the conceptions which we have. And you may wonder how a system so decentralized, without legislature or courts for much of its history, could impose obligations, all directed toward a common end. The answer, I think, is that then, just as today, society was held together not by judges and laws and soldiers, but by custom. The terms of feudal relationships were fixed not by contract or by statutes, but by custom. While violation of a custom was, after a while, in England at least, actionable before the courts, the sanction came mainly from the knowledge that the neighbors would put the screws on a continuous violator of obligations. People who did that sort of thing were striking at the very heart of the system and were destructive to the interests of everybody.

Now that, in very rough outline, was the system which furnished the social order of Europe for almost a thousand years. It had plenty of incidents which we should regard as outrageous, incidents which would not be tolerated today. But any system which can order the affairs of people for a thousand years is entitled to respect.

It is entitled particularly to respect today because it grew out of the need of people for security in a world where no security appeared. Civilization had broken down—one of the great civilizations. In the chaos which followed, this rough and realistic human

# Some Social Factors in Legal Change

institution was built up; and it served for a thousand years. So I refer to it, not because I think it was ideal, or would be possible today, but because I think anything that worked so long can teach us much.

Our present legal system arose under conditions almost diametrically opposite. Three hundred years ago there were on these shores a few thousand people. After the initial difficulties of establishing settlements, these people found themselves in the presence of unlimited space and resources; they found no enemy to disturb them, and they set themselves to the task of conquering the wilderness, and exploiting its incredible richness.

There was little that a man in that situation could call on society to do for him; all he wanted of it was to be left alone. There were certain unprofitable duties that the government could well perform: it could build roads; it could carry the mails; it could send out troops if the Indians got too obstreperous. But that was about all it could do for or with the individual.

There were some early attempts to carry out imperial policies, to restrict the efforts of individuals to acquire, to own, and to exploit. But those failed. There were also some efforts by wealthier colonists to keep people who had been brought over here to labor for others in that situation. But, with the whole continent before anyone would work for himself, those efforts were futile. And so it became, very early, the predominant idea of this community that the ownership and development of one's own property was the fundamental activity of man.

## This Vast External Realm

We are not surprised to read in the Virginia Declaration of Rights that the inherent right of man is "the enjoyment of life and liberty, with the means of acquiring and possessing property," nor to find a framer of the Constitution saying that "property is certainly the principal object of society." Americans asserted other rights: the right to assemble, the right to vote, and the other religious, civil, and political liberties. But underlying all of them was the interest in acquiring and owning property. The assertion of civil and political liberties during our Revolutionary period was not by propertyless people. It was by property owners, large and small, whose basic objection was to the impingements of a distant government upon their right to acquire and to own.

This conception of the sanctity of gathering wealth was spurred on by religion and philosophy. Deeply rooted in Puritanism was the conception that the acquisition of property was synonymous with virtue. The Puritan prophets taught lessons of thrift, honesty, and self-reliance. During the early period of our history we hear little of the virtues which were preached in the Middle Ages, little talk of faith, patience, good works, and charity. The virtues which were stressed were the rugged virtues of acquisition, thrift, honesty, and self-reliance.

The same word came from the philosophers. The political economists of the nineteenth century taught, to use a phrase of Justice Holmes, that men were not fools for doing what they already wanted to do. In the apparently discordant notes of private interest they found a symphony of public good. The Industrial Revolution opened new fields for exploitation and acquisition. The right of the individual to acquire and to do what he pleased with his own appeared to be essential to the unfolding of a universal plan.

As the century wore on, this conception became the special concern of the law, because it was the special concern of the people. Property was the thing with which people were dealing, for which they were striving. Out of all this dealing with property there flowered the concept of ownership: the right to complete dominion, the privilege of doing as one pleased with one's property. And very early in the century we hear rumblings of the idea that the liberty to use property is not a mere enactment of law, like a statute or judicial decision, but is one of those natural rights which is protected by the fundamental law of the land. It is not long before we find that not only is the idea of ownership fully imbedded in the law, but that it is beyond the reach of legislatures and beyond the reach of courts; it is enshrined in the Constitution.

It is true that throughout this development notes of doubt were sounded; but they left no echo.

In 1864, in Baltimore, speaking at the Sanitary Fair, President Lincoln said:

The world has never had a good definition of the word "liberty," and the American people just now are much in want of one. We all declare for liberty, but in using the same word we do not all mean the same thing. With some the word "liberty" may mean freedom for every man to do as he pleases with himself and the products of his labor; while with others the same word may mean the right for some men to do as they please with other men and with the product of other men's labor.

A few years before, John Stuart Mill uttered what John Morley calls an audacious doubt. He said: "Hitherto, it is questionable if all the mechanical inventions yet made have lightened the toil of any human being."

These notes, I say, left no echo. Instead, as the twentieth century approached, there grew up what we may call the American dream.

The American dream, I think, was that within this system every man could become an owner. If a man was not an owner, he was a potential owner. We heard about the Astors, the Hills, and the Rockefellers. It has been said that every soldier of Napoleon carried in his knapsack a marshal's baton, and in the early days of this century it seems to have been thought that every young American carried in his lunch box a roll of ticker tape. That was the idea with which the century opened.

Any dividing date is always an illusion, but I think for these purposes we can say that the depression was a period of such dramatic power that it made us suddenly conscious of changes of which we had all been unconsciously aware for a long time.

When that cataclysm came, with millions of people out of work, without food, we saw our dreams dissolve. We saw the situation more nearly as it was. We saw—in addition to the obvious picture of the millions who were not included in the system, who could accumulate no stores against such years of famine—we saw first of all, I think, that this system, which was based upon the uncontrolled freedom of the individual to use property for his own purposes, was headed, through the mechanism of the trade cycle, down the road to suicide.

We saw too that in the field of agriculture the individual pursuit of private interest was not adequate to care for what was suddenly revealed as a social institution. We had talked about the farm as though it were a factory. We suddenly discovered that it was not; that we were dealing with, not merely an agency of production, but a social institution.

We found, too, that over the past century not only had the population increased, with all the difficulties which that brings, but that the increase was in the number and the proportion of people who did not own property—that is, people whose primary interest in the property with which they dealt was not that of ownership. We found also that the interests of those people in that property were not recognized in any way in our legal order. Law was concerned with conceptions of ownership; these other relations to property found no place whatever.

Perhaps most important of all, we awoke to the enormous significance of universal suffrage. We discovered that in the intervening century those people who were not connected with property by ownership had acquired political power. Not only had they acquired power, but they knew it.

This situation, brought dramatically home to us by

the experiences of the past few years, should, I think, convince us that we are face to face with a demand which, from being a mere matter of humanitarian concern, has become the most pressing of political and legal problems. This demand is that our legal system shall recognize that people who are not owners, as well as those who are owners, have interests in property and in the use of property which must be considered and protected. These interests I should briefly outline in this way:

An interest in stability in the production of goods.

An interest in the use of wealth to produce and distribute goods in quantity at low cost.

An interest that the young have opportunity to form a relation to property; that is, to enter the system and get a job.

The interest of people in their job, in achieving dignity, in making it an opportunity to use their powers.

The protection of the interest in the job against arbitrary dismissal.

And, finally, security against the inevitable hazards of life—unemployment, sickness, accident, old age, death.

Those are the interests which people are demanding shall be recognized by the legal order, by legislation, by court decision, and by executive order. They are reasonable demands. They are backed with political power.

What these demands really mean is that property must be held in the medieval sense of which I spoke at the outset—not subject to absolute dominion, but conditioned upon the performance of social duties.

If we look about us, I think that we can see the outlines of the social duties which will be imposed upon the holding and use of property. The interest of people in stability in the production of goods seems to be in process of recognition in the regulation and control of investment funds. The idea of some control in this field is not new, as our banking laws testify. But the Securities Act of 1933, the Securities Exchange Act of 1934, and the Public Utility Act of 1935 contain a very definite extension of principle.

People have come to believe that the hazards of great expansion and contraction of credit and capital are immeasurably increased when individual freedom to use capital for improvement or speculation is given free rein. They believe that there are social duties, if only negative ones, which if not privately recognized must be enforced by the Government.

A great deal of what is being done through the Securities and Exchange Commission is pure policing —a more effective preventive of fraud than we had before. But I do not think that is the significant thing. The significant thing is the idea, most clearly discernible in the Public Utility Act of 1935, that while government cannot tell us how we shall invest, it can tell us how we shall *not* use our investment funds. It can prohibit certain uses of capital and credits which are regarded as anti-social.

I think that idea will be extended to other fields and the attempt will be made not only to control the rate of the formation of capital—to prevent waves of speculation or fear from upsetting it—but to prevent certain directions of investment. In the past the creation of industrial leviathans, though viewed with apprehension, was dealt with only when some evil intent or elusive result was demonstrable. Perhaps in the future the use of funds in such a venture may be forbidden, or made impossible by taxation, or, should some monster still escape, its dissolution may be required upon some simpler test of social value.

In the field of the production and distribution of goods the history of the attempt to impose social obligations is a long one. We are all accustomed to legislation regarding uniform bills of lading and weights and measures, to government grades and standards, and to pure food laws. We are also used to the idea, expressed in the Interstate Commerce Act, the Sherman Act, the Federal Trade Commission Act, and the Clayton Act, and, more recently, in the Patman Act, that certain limitations are to be put on business practices.

Recently we have all been giving opinions about the Patman Act; we have all been puzzled by it. Yet it is the legitimate descendant of the statutes which I have mentioned. The confusion in it is a family characteristic.

The early conception of restraints of trade was very simple: a monopoly raised prices and since we desire lower prices, monopoly is bad. But another conception has run somewhat at cross-purposes with that. This conception is that the large unit may eliminate the small producer or distributor, and that that is bad.

# Some Social Factors in Legal Change

The small distributor and the small producer did not want to be eliminated; and many people did not want him eliminated, not because he necessarily, or perhaps ever, brought lower prices, but because he was a social institution. He had implications in the community which were quite unrelated to price. It is that conflict of purposes, to produce low costs and prices and at the same time to prevent low prices from eliminating small producers, which is now confusing us.

In this field of compelling recognition of the social interest in increased production and lower prices I should expect not new conceptions, but rather new methods. There is a general feeling that administrative and judicial control has never been adequate. The government is always behind-hand; practices are developed and are well flowered before the government ever steps in and tries to deal with them.

It would not surprise me to see in the future a restriction of the privacy which has shrouded corporate activities. The state, which creates these legal entities as instruments for furthering the public interest, may exercise its visitorial power and subject their costs, their processes of production, and their business dealings to public study, with the idea that periodic scrutiny in and of itself would have a beneficial effect, and that attention will be drawn to situations which require correction. At first blush the lawyer may feel that this would be an unwarranted intrusion into private affairs. He may feel as Lord Melbourne did about a sermon which he heard.

"No one," said the old gentleman, "has a greater

185

respect for the church than I have, but things have come to a pretty pass when religion is allowed to invade the sphere of private life."

But the lawyer should not forget that visitorial power has been properly used for a long time in examining the affairs of financial institutions and public utilities and should bend his efforts toward assuring that if the power be extended, it be done with restraint and fairness.

Another new method of control has already been indicated in this country and abroad—occasional government competition where there is widespread popular belief that an industry has been particularly resistant to control. There may also be competition from consumer cooperatives, if people believe that sales or advertising costs have produced burdensome prices. We may find, too, an extension of the conception of a public utility to include such industries as the distribution of milk and the production of bread, where the elimination of a large number of units, necessarily wasteful, may be accompanied by regulation of service and price.

Those, I suggest, are methods by which the interests in property of people who are not owners but consumers of its products may be safeguarded.

There remain the interests in property of those who work with it, the field of labor relations—at present a word of wrath. They have already been mentioned.

I wish to stress here that they are not, as so many people assume, merely economic interests. An arbi-

# Some Social Factors in Legal Change

trary dismissal means, of course, loss of earning power, but it also arouses the same sense of outrage as the denial of a fair trial, confiscation, or the invasion of one's house without a search warrant. Our political heritage for six hundred years is one of revulsion against arbitrary treatment.

Then too, I spoke of the dignity of the job, and the oppotunity to use one's powers. You will know what the lack of that means if you recall Charley Chaplin's picture *Modern Times*. Beneath the humor of that picture there was, in reality, the industrial relation. The human being, chained to that moving belt, ceased to be a human being. There was no dignity, no peace in that life; there was no justice in that relationship, subjected to every petty tyranny of a petty tyrant with more authority than a drill sergeant, the power to deny food. We are apt to forget that the function of the industrial system is not merely to produce goods, it is to produce people. The only reason for producing goods is to keep people alive. And if in producing goods to keep the people alive we destroy the people, the whole system is futile.

The mere statement of those problems indicates, to me at least, that it is absurd to believe that the state alone can protect every interest of every worker, or that they can be left to individual bargain or benevolence. Effective organization of labor is absolutely essential. That seems to me the very first requisite. I not only think that effective organization is necessary, but I think the methods must be found to get that organization accepted by the powers of the industrial system.

# This Vast External Realm

I am not prepared to argue whether one or two organizations or three or four or how many should be recognized; that, I think, is a matter of comparative detail which will work itself out. But there are some things which seem to me clear.

One is that the state must step in to protect the right to organize. There must be no nonsense or doubt about that. We must use all the powers of the law to coerce any individual who undertakes to set up his private desire that there should not be organization against the social necessity of having it.

After that, the state must see to it that management deals with these organizations. It might well condition its aid. It might require that the unions be organized and conducted in such a way as to be representative of and responsive to their members. This would mean not only an absence of employer control, but also that by regular and fair elections the members might express their will as to policy and leadership.

To have responsible managers, and not mere underlings, deal with such organizations will make for industrial statesmanship on both sides. The mere fact that labor reaches a position of dignity will do much for the worker, and will go far to produce the leaders of industrial peace. Guerrilla warfare produces leaders for guerrilla warfare. With the coming of peace, or even a cessation of war, the demands upon leadership change and with the change a new school of leaders will emerge.

But these matters, important as they are, are merely preliminary to approaching a more fundamental question. How can we get, in this great decentralized system, common agreement on the valuation of interests in industrial property, a common consent to the mutual obligations which alone can make the system work to a common objective? That, you will see, is one reason why I have been talking about the feudal system. There, without legislatures or courts, people evolved from stark necessity, by custom and common thinking, a common consent to mutual obligations which created a system out of apparently independent, if not hostile, units. The same thing is not beyond our reach in industry. It cannot be done by coercion or by any of the parties in industry looking to outside force to overawe the other. It cannot be finally or authoritatively done at all. But much can be done by registering within industry certain rough evaluations of our present position and by marking out the fields for collective bargaining.

It should not be impossible, in some industries at least, to hold conventions or conferences, where those who work, those who invest, and those who manage are represented, to state, so far as may be done, the matters agreed upon. It would be agreed, I suppose, that all the persons interested are little ganglions within and not little gods outside the industry. Its interests are their interests. Ultimately the hopes of all for what they have bound up in it, whether it be their lives or their investment, must rest upon the industry. These hopes, these charges of human beings upon the industry, might be stated. Elementary as this sounds, it would be a great advance to have some degree of agreement upon the charges which, to the extent of its ability, an industry should meet—wages, salaries, interest, charges for accident, sickness, unemployment and old-age insurance, dividends. It would be a tremendous advance to recognize that these interests can be secured only by the assumption of mutual obligations. It would be the greatest advance of all to have the persons concerned recognize that the problems were theirs to be worked out, if at all, by them.

There are other matters on which all parties are, or should be, ready to state some common ground. We know enough about the physiological and psychological effects of fatigue and monotony to agree that some periods of rest in the year and in the day are necessary. The lunch period is not, for instance, a mere feeding time. We know too that all has not been said on the subject of dismissal when we quote legal language to the effect that an employment may be terminated at will for any reason or no reason. Dismissal is the supreme economic penalty. It should not be imposed for a trivial cause. If it is imposed should not the industry, through a dismissal allowance, share the burden of the inevitable period of unemployment?

Finally, we need some method of having the people immediately concerned evolve a law industrial, like the old law merchant, by which collective agreements may achieve some binding effect recognized by the parties to them. This cannot be imposed from outside; it must evolve from within industry.

Here, I believe are the objects of collective bargaining and here is a method of furthering it, more fruitful than focusing the efforts of all upon the politics of power. That road leads only to a conflict of increasing bitterness, in which finally all objectives disappear except the extermination of the opponent. If we keep before us the objects of bargaining and remember that there is no more to bargain for than we produce, we become realistic. If from time to time we state our grounds of agreement instead of meeting only when we disagree, we keep our tempers. If we learn the art of yielding what must be yielded to the changing present we can save the best of the past.

I do not present these sketchy observations as a blueprint of the future. They are merely suggestions of lines along which the art of yielding might usefully be employed. In speaking of a critical period in Roman history Lord Acton said:

> The old and famous aristocracy of birth and rank had made a stubborn resistance but it knew the art of yielding. The later and more selfish aristocracy was unable to learn it. The character of the people was changed by the sterner motives of dispute. The fight for political power had been carried on with the moderation which is so honorable a quality of party contests in England. But the struggle for the objects of material existence grew to be as ferocious as civil controversies in France. Repulsed by the rich . . . the people, three hundred and twenty thousand of whom depended on public rations for food, were ready to follow any man who promised to obtain for them by revolution what they could not obtain by law.

For the bar, the art of yielding lies in yielding our preconceptions. The problems ahead are not beyond our capacity if we will give our minds freedom to deal with them. But if we see in every social question only the seeds of Götterdämerung, if all our boasted inventiveness turns to the dust of constitutional platitudes and the formulae of dead economists, then we shall be a menace to the very social order we affect to defend and become the instruments of social catastrophe.

# The Responsibility for
# Decision in Foreign Policy

In giving one's reflections on "The Responsibility for Decision in Foreign Policy" two lines of thought occur. One concerns the importance of decisiveness in conducting foreign relations, the effect of indecision, or no decision, or contradictory decisions. The other relates to the body or person upon whom rests the final responsibility for making the decisions which determine our course as a nation, and how this task is or should be performed. Both lines start from a common point—where the responsibility and authority lie.

In our American system the President is the person charged with the heavy duty of giving us the line to follow in our dealings with other nations. But, wholly

From *The Yale Review*, Vol. XLIV, No. 1 (September 1954).

apart from constitutional and legal considerations, his will is not given unlimited scope. In the first place, he is making decisions about our relations with foreign nations—countries, areas, peoples outside of the United States where our laws do not govern and our writ does not run, where the preconceptions of American life are not taken for granted—in short, that vast portion of the earth's surface where Americans are foreigners. The very idea requires the enlightenment which came to the old mountaineer who took his first train ride from his Appalachian crossroads to town, with his face pressed against the window. When the train stopped, he heaved a deep sigh and said to his companion, "John, there's a heap of folks between here and home, and I guess, by God, we ain't seen half of 'em."

Here is the beginning of understanding of foreign affairs.

It is amid the manifold complexities of the relations between the external world and our own by-no-means-simple country that the President must lay down the line to follow. Whether we, his fellow citizens, follow it or not is another matter. And this suggests the second factor qualifying the freedom of the President's will in reaching his decisions. He is deciding for this particular country at a particular time and under particular circumstances. So there is involved the kind of country and people he leads—the sort of ideas we have inherited and now hold, our traditions and affiliations, our physical resources and the use to which we are putting them and are capable of putting them. All these elements narrow and affect the course of decisions, as currrents, winds, shoals, and land affect the decisions of the mariner.

But to return to our point, the final responsibility for decision lies with the President. Sometimes confusion arises about this. We hear it said that the National Security Council is to make, or has made, some important decision. This is an illusion, and a most troublesome one. The NSC decides nothing. It is merely a mechanism for preparing and presenting matters for the President's decision. The power and the responsibility lie with him. He can accept, modify, reject, or do nothing with recommendations from the Council, which is merely a meeting of certain of his advisers. If he does nothing, no decision is made, or a decision to do nothing is made by default. However much the Council's staff is elaborated, it remains a forum—and one which can be very useful—for determining the main problems which require decision and for presenting recommendations to the President.

Again, one reads from time to time that at some meeting with "leaders on the Hill" this or that matter of foreign policy was "decided." This, too, I believe, involves a misconception. These meetings produce not so much a decision of policy as opinions as to whether or how a particular proposal or decision in which Congressional action will be needed can be carried out. Again the responsibility for deciding whether or how to go ahead rests with the President.

It is placed there by the Constitution and confirmed by a century and three-quarters of experience. The Presidential system supported by the separation of powers is the special American contribution to the science and art of government. It is a contribution which presents its problems, which calls for strong and decisive leadership, but which, given such leadership, has served the country well. Under it the President, the only official in the country elected by all the people, the leader of the dominant political party, the chief magistrate, is the head. His cabinet officers, the chiefs of the departments of government, are selected by him, hold their tenure at his pleasure, and are advisers to him. They can be effective only through him and with his support.

Attempts to graft onto this system institutions and practices drawn from the cabinet of parliamentary systems are usually a mistake and can be mischievous. No good comes from attempts to dilute, share, or usurp the authority and responsibility of the President.

While no good comes from attempts to invade the authority and responsibility of the President, they are continually made and sometimes succeed. This occurs under weak Presidents. The result is Congressional government, which, in turn, results, under twentieth-century conditions, in a negative and vacillating foreign policy, the impairment of our world position, and danger to our national safety. This situation has been described by a former colleague as the "Frenchification" of the Constitution. By this he means government where power is centered in a national assembly as in the four French republican constitutions. Under this system, the Presidency tends to become ceremonial, executive power virtually disappears, and authority is assumed by parliamentarians, undisciplined by any penalty for repudiating the executive, divided into numerous groups no one of which commands decisive power, and unable and unequipped to lead the country in a sustained, complex, and difficult course of action. The foreign policy emerging from such a situation is formed by slogans and emotion; decisions represent the lowest common denominator of the groups in the legislative assembly. The vital issues, which are always painful, are evaded and decision postponed until events decide them.

We are familiar enough with this course of events as it has appeared and reappeared in French history from the First Republic to the Fourth. But perhaps we do not understand how closely our own situation approximates the French when the Presidential powers fall from hands not strong enough to wield them. For these powers are not self-executing. They cannot be exercised by a committee. They reside in and depend upon the quality of one man. This has been stated by one who held and knew how to use them:

> Many diverse elements entered into the creation of the office, springing, as it did, from the parent idea of the separation of powers.
> There was the firm conviction of such powerful and shrewd minds as that of John Adams that the greatest protection against unlimited power lay in an executive secured against the encroachments of a national assembly. Then there were the fears of those who suspected a plot to establish a monarchy on these shores. Others believed that the experience under the Confederation

showed above all the need of stability through a strong central administration. Finally, there was the need for compromise among these and many other views.

The result was a compromise—a compromise which that shrewd observer, Alexis de Tocqueville, over a hundred and twenty years ago, believed would not work. He thought that the Presidential office was too weak. The President, he thought, was at the mercy of Congress. The President could recommend, to be sure, but he had no power and the Congress had. The Congress could disregard his recommendations, overrule his vetoes, reject his nominations. De Tocqueville thought that no man of parts, worthy of leadership, would accept so feeble a role.

This was not a foolish view and there was much in our early history which tended to bear it out. But there is a power in the course of events which plays its own part. In this case again, Justice Holmes's epigram proved true. He said a page of history is worth a whole volume of logic. And as the pages of history were written they unfolded powers in the Presidency not explicitly found in Article II of the Constitution.

In the first place, the President became the leader of a political party. The party under his leadership had to be dominant enough to put him in office. This political party leadership was the last thing the Constitution contemplated. The President's election was not intended to be mixed up in the hurly-burly of partisan politics. . . . The people were to choose wise and respected men who would meet in calm seclusion and choose a President. The runner-up would be Vice President.

All of this went by the board—though most of the original language remains in the Constitution. Out of the struggle and tumult of the political arena a new and different President emerged—the man who led a political party to victory and retained in his hands the power of party leadership. That is, he retained it, like the sword Excalibur, if he could wrest it from the scabbard and wield it.

Another development was connected with the first. As the President came to be elected by the whole people, he became responsible to the whole people. . . . Our whole people looked to him for leadership, and not confined within the limits of a written document. Every hope and every fear of his fellow citizens, almost every aspect of their welfare and activity, falls within the scope of his concern—indeed, falls within the scope of his duty. Only one who has held that office can really appreciate that. It is the President's responsibility to look at all questions from the point of view of the whole people. His written and spoken word commands national—often international—attention.

These powers which are not explicitly written into the Constitution are powers which no President can pass on to his successor. They go only to him who can take and use them.[1]

We have had Presidents who have not exercised the Presidential power. It will not exhaust the list to mention Presidents Pierce, Buchanan, Grant, Harding, and Coolidge. When Presidential default occurs it is not correct to say that Congress steps into the vacant place. Attempts are made to do so, but they cannot fully succeed since Congress is not designed, organized, or equipped for executive leadership.

Aside from the obvious reason that so large a body,

1. Harry S. Truman, *The New York Times,* May 9, 1954.

designed to be a check upon action, cannot be the leader in action, there is another reason highly relevant to our present inquiry. It is that our two-party system cloaks a multi-party reality. There is a saying—not wholly accurate—that strict party votes occur only on the organization of the House and Senate. But it is true that strict party votes are rare enough to cause considerable comment. Every newspaper reader knows that across the traditional party lines run perhaps even deeper alignments—the farm bloc, the protectionist bloc, the isolationist group, the Southern group (on certain questions), the "liberal group" (on certain questions), the mountain states (on minerals and wool), the public power group, the economy group, and so on.

The conclusion relevant here is that a party leader in Congress is not a leader, so far as foreign affairs is concerned, qualified to speak for the party which he nominally leads. His view is not accepted as any more important or controlling than that of any other member. In the absence of Presidential leadership, congressional policy must be evolved by negotiation among the groups and with a high appreciation of short-term electoral approval. These conditions are not favorable to understanding or dealing with fundamental realities and issues or to producing continuity of policy and the sober facing of difficult problems requiring costly sacrifices. The Nye Committee did not provide the country with an understanding of the problems left by the First World War or with policies consistent with the security of the United States. It resulted in a

# The Responsibility for Decision

withdrawal into "Fortress America" which was no fortress at all, because the incidence of power pressures occurred outside it. And it is there—where the pressures focus—that the United States must exercise its capacity to mold and shape the future.

So we return to the President as the pivotal point, the critical element in reaching decisions on foreign policy. Now the capacity to decide is not a common attribute of mankind. It becomes increasingly rare as the difficulty of the problems increases. The choice becomes one between courses all of which are hard and dangerous. The "right" one, if there is a right one, is quite apt to be the most immediately difficult one. It was certainly so in reaching a decision regarding Korea in June, 1950. In these cases the mind tends to remain suspended between alternatives and to seek escape by postponing the issue. There are always persuasive advocates of opposing courses. "On the one hand" balances "on the other." The problem itself becomes the enemy.

General Marshall understands this very well. Many a time he would burst out in an interminable discussion with: "Gentlemen, don't fight the question. Decide it." And he has often observed that the rarest of all gifts is the capacity for decision.

Many men and some Presidents don't have it. And when this occurs, the consequences are irreparable. It is one of the maladies for which there is no cure, except amputation.

Some years ago a lawyer friend received a call from a man who thanked him for giving him the best advice he had ever received. "You did not take my case," the man explained. "You listened to me, and you said, 'My friend, you are in one hell of a fix.' And," he added, "I was."

So is the country when the function of decision in foreign policy breaks down. For the inescapable result is drift. And it is drift away from the association, the coalition, of free nations which cannot exist without us, and without which we cannot exist as the nation all of us have known. And it is drift in this direction not necessarily from desire—many members of Congress desire quite the opposite—but because policy in association or coalition requires a vast number of co-ordinated and continuous actions which, for the reasons given, Congress without vigorous executive leadership is not able to provide. This vigorous leadership often involves conflict and competing appeals to the people, the common source of power. This is inherent in the system of the separation of powers, the framers of which did not rate harmony between the executive and legislative branches as highly as some of their successors.

Different Presidents have gone about reaching conclusions and decisions for the conduct of foreign relations in different ways. Some have relied heavily on solitary reflection and study. One can see instances of this in Presidents Jefferson, Lincoln, and Wilson. Some have relied substantially upon advisers not in the established chart of organization. Here one might cite the two Roosevelts. Others have been meticulous in sticking to "channels," of whom President Truman

# The Responsibility for Decision

is outstanding. But, however he works, the President must be free to choose the methods most suited to him. He cannot be confined. Particularly, he must not be confined by law. Legislation that a President must consult this, that, or the other person or body will be futile and harmful. He can be given facilities, but he cannot be compelled to use them.

But it can properly be said that some courses are apt to be more successful than others. Successful organization and method will recognize two fundamental truths—the indivisibility of policy and the speciality of the foreign field.

Governmental policy is an integer—political policy, diplomatic, military, economic, fiscal. It is all one. Each depends upon, is stimulated and limited by the others. The history of our government decisions in the year 1950 is a clinic for any who wish to spell out this thesis. But it will hardly be disputed in theory, while it is very apt to be disregarded in practice. And there will always be argument about the hierarchy of importance. Do we cut the cloth according to the pattern? And where do we find the pattern? But the first requirement is that there must be a pattern.

While this is true, it is also true that, despite popular belief, the field of foreign affairs is a field of special competence. Those who have spent their lives in the study of foreign nations and peoples know more about them than those who have not, just as physicians or physicists know more about their fields of special study. They often make mistakes, and bad ones. We are under no compulsion to take their advice. But, where our lives are at stake, as between tossing a coin and consulting the specialists, we would be wise to do the latter.

Now it is an interesting fact that the Secretary of State is the senior member of the Cabinet. He is the senior member because this Cabinet office was the first to be created upon the formation of our government. And it was the first to be created because then, as now, our relations with foreign nations were the most pressing of all problems with which our government had to deal. This has not always been true in the years which intervened. But it was true then, and it is true now.

Whatever primacy one attaches to our relations with the world beyond our borders, it is plain that a President needs continuous and knowledgeable advice about them. The Department of State exists for this purpose, is highly competent to perform it, and should be the principal, unifying, and final source of advice and recommendation. Unifying and final in this sense, that reports and recommendations from all sources, official and unofficial, come to the President—some of them good, more of them plausible. All of these should be referred to and reported on by the Department of State, which must live with the problem. Its view may be rejected, but it should be heard.

So far we have spoken of a "department" and about "its" view. But a department is made up of thousands of people. It cannot advise the President. And it rarely has *a* view. Here enters the Secretary of State—an unenviable figure. As Henry Adams pointed out, he is destined to be a pariah with the Congress because he represents problems which the Congress wishes to forget. Votes can be lost but not gained through foreign policy.

Nevertheless he has a place, and an important one, in the making of decisions. It is not the one most photographed and publicized—his exhausting flights to conferences, his greeting of visiting dignitaries, his appearance before committees of Congress and the public as a spokesman for the Administration. His other and essential role concerns both the special knowledge of the foreign field and the synthesis of foreign policy into a unified governmental policy.

In the first aspect he must draw from the Department of State in usable form its full knowledge and wisdom upon the many matters which press for decision. He should distrust conclusions, his own or others', when they provide answers too facile and pat, but should rather spur and encourage his departmental colleagues to bring together all their varied knowledge and points of view so that all possibilities are tested against the most stringent criticism. He must keep them headed into the problem and present to them the other governmental factors involved which fall outside their field of special competence, but which must weigh heavily with the President.

Out of this method of work will come recommendations from the foreign affairs point of view influenced by, but not wholly coordinated with, the limiting factors of our capabilities in the economic, fiscal, military, and domestic political fields. This final reconciliation must be made by the President. He should be kept fully informed of the progress of the work so that issues are not presented to him suddenly and at a late stage when choices have narrowed, and so that the President's thought may be fully reflected in the work of preparation. But, before the matter comes to the President for action, much can be done to assure that all his advisers have understood and considered one another's points of view and the whole scope of limitations and capabilities applicable to the problem.

Much of this is accomplished by consultation between cabinet colleagues and through such valuable interdepartmental machinery as the National Advisory Council on financial matters and the National Security Council on security matters. It would unduly extend this article to go into these established channels for coordinating policy. But one matter should be mentioned which defies formal organization, but which is absolutely essential. It concerns habits of work and confidence and collaboration between officers of different departments.

One of the curious and toughly resistant characteristics of government departments is the tendency of their people to isolate themselves from other departments and to regard persons outside their ranks with something amounting, on occasion, to suspicion and hostility. It may seem extraordinary, but it is nevertheless true, that not until General Marshall's tenure as Secretary of Defense had the Secretary of State and his senior officers met with the Secretary of Defense and Joint Chiefs of Staff for continuous discussion and development of policy. And yet foreign policy and

# The Responsibility for Decision

military policy divorced from one another are both operating in the field of phantasy.

From September, 1950, until January, 1953—I am not informed thereafter—officers of the two departments worked in the closest and most loyal cooperation and greatly to the public good. This does not happen automatically; it requires constant attention and effort from all concerned and especially from the top. For both departments have internal differences springing from perfectly proper differences of emphasis and interests, either from the services, in one case, or the geographical divisions, in the other. Both desire to keep their differences within the family. But it is useful and often most productive to bring them out in discussion, provided those in the discussion preserve confidence. The value of these years of common work in mutual enlightenment, confidence, and advancement of policy and action cannot be overstated.

The same relationship existed with the Economic Cooperation Administration and with its successor, the Mutual Security Agency, and to a lesser, but useful, degree with other Departments having functions in the foreign field—Treasury, Commerce, Agriculture, and Labor.

The purpose of all this was not necessarily to get agreed recommendations and papers, but to get understanding; and, where there were differences, to have them brought out, not covered up, and to have them intelligent and intelligible differences. One can always get an agreed paper by increasing the vagueness and generality of its statements. The staff of any interdepartmental committee has a fatal weakness for this type of agreement by exhaustion. But such agreements are no good and of no service to the President, if he has the capacity for decision. What he needs to know are the real issues, honestly presented, with extraneous matter stripped away.

We come back then to where we started—to the President. The decisions are his. Helped by his departmental advisers and their staffs, helped by his own Executive Office—the Bureau of the Budget, the Economic Advisers, and so forth—ultimately he must decide. The volume of work which should be done is appalling. It cannot be got through by listening to oral presentations, or "briefings," or reading one-page memoranda. It has to be sweated out. The facts have to be mastered, the choices and their consequences understood—so far as consequences can be understood; and then upon "judgments and intuitions more subtle than any articulate major premise" the decision made.

# Legislative-Executive Relations

This centennial year of Woodrow Wilson's birth should not pass without a glance at the current aspect of some of the problems discussed in his first, and perhaps best, book, *Congressional Government*. When it appeared, Gamaliel Bradford wrote: "We have no hesitation in saying that this is one of the most important books, dealing with political subjects, which have ever issued from the American press." In the next fifteen years it went through fifteen editions.

One who reads the book seventy years later comes to the same conclusion as Bradford. It is a most important and penetrating book. And yet over it hangs an atmosphere of melancholy and of irony. Of melancholy, because, as Wilson's biographer says, "in the end, it is scarcely too much to say, he fell a victim to the defects [in the Constitutional structure] he had so clearly

From *The Yale Review*, Vol. XLV, No. 4 (June 1956).

perceived." Of irony, because one of the central themes, the decline of the Presidency, was to be conclusively disapproved by Woodrow Wilson, twenty-eighth President of the United States.

The theme of the book is that Congress is the central and predominant power in our governmental system, and a discussion of what is necessary, in the author's judgment, to make that power fully effective and responsible.

The argument may be briefly outlined. In practice "the literary theory" of the Constitution had broken down. "While we have been shielding it from criticism it has slipped away from us." This was a theory of checks and balances—of which John Adams found eight in writing to John Tyler. Chiefly they were the balance of the state governments and the people against the Federal Government; and, within the latter, the separation and mutual checks of the legislative, executive, and judicial powers. But out of a century of developing a continent and out of a civil war, the Federal had emerged, visible to every citizen, as "the greater and more sovereign power." The doctrine of implied powers under the Constitution was the legal instrument of this achievement. Within the Federal Government the judicial power ceased to be a real check and balance to the legislature once it had "declared itself without authority to question the legislature's privilege of determining the nature and extent of its own powers in the choice of means for giving effect to its constitutional prerogatives." And that other theoretical check, the executive, had proved ineffective because the power of the Presidency had waned, "fallen from its first estate of dignity" in the early days of the Republic, as the power of Congress in the test of action became predominant.

The bulk of the book, and its abiding value, is an analysis and description of Congress and its operation. Here the weakness discerned was in leadership and responsibility, because in practice both had been diffused through the committee system. The young author found the path of progress in the direction of the parliamentary system where authority, party leadership, and responsibility for governmental action might be joined. As the years went by, he was to come to a different conclusion.

It is, I know, fashionable to state that in the seventy years since Wilson wrote there has been so great and steady a growth of presidential power that the constitutional problem of today is the checking of executive aggrandizement. I do not share this view. True, the power, prestige, and—most certainly—the responsibilities of the Presidency have grown greatly. But the growth of power has not been steady or maintained. Presidential power is great in times of war, national emergency (such as the depression), or when the sense of danger from abroad is acute. But when a consciousness of security, normalcy, and prosperity (whether well-founded or not) dominates, the power of the office, as a means of positive accomplishment, diminishes in competition with the multitudinous and often inconsistent appeals .of congressional leaders. Furthermore, any idea that the contestants put into the arena by the Constitution are ill-matched in power and resources is far from the fact. The question, in my judgment, is whether the checking and balancing prescribed by the Constitution is so conducted as to permit a continuity of policy, involving over a period of years the maintenance of distasteful measures. For this is essential if we and our friends are to maintain our position and safety in competition with powers of unmistakable capacity for consistent and sustained effort. I believe that it is possible to do this only if the presidential office is made and maintained strong and resolute.

The central question is not whether the Congress should be stronger than the Presidency, or vice versa; but, how the Congress and the Presidency can both be strengthened to do the pressing work that falls to each to do, and to both to do together.

When one speaks of the executive working with the Congress, one is using shorthand. The center and focus of legislative-executive relations lie in the congressional committees and in the method of their operation. Much as the President and his associates may influence the Congress through direct appeal to the people, the route from planning to action leads through the committees to legislation. For today nearly all programs require funds, authority, and men, which Congress may grant, skimp, or withhold. Legislation is more than the "oil of government"; it is the essential prerequisite of government. And it is in the committees, where Congress is least susceptible to party discipline, that it gives its legislative answer to the policies of the administration.

There is another fact, also, which must not escape us. While each one of these committees and subcommittees is a channel along which influence may flow from Congress to the executive, it is quite possible for influence to flow in the other direction along the same channels. If it were not so, our government would be almost impossible to operate. To be sure, Congress has its defences. Unless an executive officer or employee wishes to risk a year of penitential reverie, he had best not use any appropriated funds to "pay for any personal service, advertisement, telegram, telephone, letter, printed or written matter, or other device, intended or designed to influence in any manner a member of Congress, to favor or oppose, by vote or otherwise, any legislation or appropriation by Congress, whether before or after the introduction of any bill or resolution. . . ."

And, as Wilson pointed out, consultation with the Senate has a tendency to be all one way. "The President really has no voice at all in the conclusions of the Senate with a reference to his diplomatic transactions . . . and yet without a voice in the conclusion there is no consultation. . . ." "The Senate," he adds, "when it closes its doors, upon going into 'executive session,' closes them upon the President as much as upon the rest of the world." There is truth in this— bitter truth, as President Wilson, lying on his sickbed while the Senate formulated reservations to the League of Nations Covenant, was to experience. But Wilson overstates the isolation of the Hill and the White House from one another, just as he does when he writes, "His [the President's] only power of compelling compliance on the part of the Senate lies in his initiative in negotiation, which affords him a chance to get the country into such scrapes, so pledged in the view of the world to certain courses of action, that the Senate hesitates to bring about the appearance of dishonor which would follow its refusal to ratify the rash promises or to support the indiscreet threats of the Department of State." If, for instance, one studies the interplay of influence between the Department and the committees on the Formosa Treaty and legislation of 1955, one can see the bearing of this last observation. Nonetheless, one must conclude, I think, that in the evolution of policy comprised in these measures, the Department and the committees each deeply influenced the other.

In the process of communication and mutual effort to influence between the committees and the executive a simple, prosaic, but deeply important fact stands out. The process takes a great deal of time and effort. It is obvious, too, that while there are many committees and subcommittees, there is only one Secretary in each department; and the committees, quite naturally, want to discuss important matters with the Secretary. On his part, the Secretary knows that he must do this, and do it effectively, if the policies of the administration are to be carried out. So the time spent in congressional meetings is spent—and, for the most part, well spent—in the performance of one of his most important duties. It is possible, I think, to arrive at a quantitative estimate of the time this duty requires.

On November 29, 1955, Secretary Dulles told us that he had met during his tenure of office "more than a hundred times with bipartisan congressional groups." This seems to me quite normal practice. As nearly as I can reconstruct it from my appointment books, I met during four years as Secretary on 214 occasions with these groups. One hundred and twenty-five of these were formal committee meetings, usually stenographically reported. The remainder were informal meetings. Many committee meetings occupied half a day, measured from the Secretary's portal-to-portal (if more, each half-day is counted as a meeting). Informal meetings were usually shorter, running from an hour to two or three. In my experience preparation for meetings required at least as much time as the meetings themselves, usually more, since the ground which would be covered was never precisely predictable. I will not be far wrong, then, in estimating that each formal meeting took half a day and preparation half a day, or a total of 125 days; that each informal meeting took about one-quarter of a day. This is in the neighborhood of one-sixth of my working days in Washington. Periods of absence on international conferences are excluded. There were, of course, additional and more relaxed opportunities for exchange of views on social occasions after working hours.

General figures cannot reflect the peaks of pressure which the work with Congress involves. There are occasions when, not a sixth of the Secretary's time, but all of it is occupied on the Hill. For instance, from June 1, 1951, to June 9, inclusive, I testified every day except Sunday and nearly all day before the joint Senate committees investigating the relief of General MacArthur. Preparation began on May 8, with work, at the outset, chiefly at night, and continued every day until it filled pretty much the whole day. With these hearings, concluded, I began preparation on June 22 for hearings before the House Committee on Foreign Affairs on the $8.5 billion foreign aid bill. The actual hearings occupied June 26, 27, and 28. So for this seven-week period, from May 11 to the end of June, fully half of the Secretary's time and energy was spent on work with congressional committees.

July and August 1949 present an example of diversity of matters crowded, indeed jumbled, together in a short time. July was the month of the publication of the China White Paper. It began with discussion with a number of individual Senators and Congressmen interested in Chinese questions. These went on through the month. On the twentieth and again on the twenty-seventh were lengthy meetings with the Joint Atomic Energy Committee in an attempt to clear the way for an improvement in our working relations in this field with Great Britain and Canada. Due to leaks and distorted publicity the effort failed. The twenty-eighth was taken up with hearings on the military assistance program before the House Foreign Affairs Committee; and on the twenty-ninth with preliminary discussion of the subject with the Chairman of the Senate Foreign Relations and Armed Services

Committees. On August 2 I appeared before a joint meeting of these committees in the morning, returning to the House Committee in the afternoon. After a conference with Chairmen Connally and Kee on August 4, the discussion with the joint Senate committees was resumed on the morning of the fifth, and that with the House committee in the afternoon. Public hearings before the joint Senate committees took the morning of the eighth. I met President Quirino of the Philippines, who arrived in the afternoon, and talked with him on the ninth. The morning of the tenth was given over to an appearance before the House Foreign Affairs Committee on the White Paper, and the morning of the eleventh to another meeting on military assistance. After two meetings on the twelfth with Senator Vandenberg, I was able to turn to other than congressional matters until the end of the month, when the President and I met with Senators George and Lucas to discuss problems raised by the Reciprocal Trade Agreements Bill.

January 1950 was another active month, with fifteen meetings, seven committee appearances, and eight informal meetings. The subjects covered included Formosa, complete surveys of our foreign relations, the departmental budget for 1951, aid to China, the Selective Service Bill, the All-American canal in the Southwest, Korea, and an appointment in which a member of Congress was interested.

In all these hours and days of meetings and consultations, as in all work, the moments of positive accomplishment, of forward movement, are disappoint-

217

ingly few. Much of the time is spent in what Secretary Stimson used to call "stopping rat holes." But that, too, is important work—as one finds out when it is neglected—even though it leaves the big tasks untouched. For instance, when Mr. Attlee came here in December 1950 apprehension was expressed in the Senate that he and the President might enter into secret arrangements. Indeed, Senator Kem, for himself and twenty-three Republican Senators, introduced a resolution giving it as the sense of the Senate that the President at the close of the meetings should make a full and complete report on them to the Senate and that he should not enter into any understandings or agreements which might bind the United States. This plainly was an infringement of the constitutional prerogative of the President to conduct negotiations with foreign nations. In this case the issue was an unreal one, since it has become customary for the Secretary of State to meet with the foreign committee of each house after important international meetings and review developments with them. So on December 9 I attended a joint meeting of the two committees and discussed with them most amicably all that had taken place. Interest in the resolution was shortlived. On December 18, 1950, it was defeated by a vote of 45 to 30.

These congressional meetings before and after an international conference, useful as they are, have a disadvantage which is part of the great glare of publicity thrown on all preparation for these conferences as well as upon the conferences themselves. Flexibility even in minor matters is much more difficult when, before a meeting, all possibilities are analyzed in public and positions publicly taken. Agreement requires that some, perhaps all, modify their attitudes to meet changes by others. A position publicly proclaimed is more rigid by reason of its public nature. Furthermore, to announce all one's positions in advance of the negotiation is apt to make it merely a forum for reiterating final positions and not a true negotiation. But there are so many contributors to this situation that it would be unfair to attribute much of it to the liaison with Congress.

The occasions when the executive and the Congress are brought together in the origination or the development of policy are not found in these executive, and certainly not in the public, sessions of congressional committees. The latter have an important and useful place in the democratic governmental process. But it is in the public examination and criticism of proposed action. This both tests what is proposed, and, through press, radio, and television coverage, informs the electorate in regard to it. The creative process is both more individual and more elusive because more private. And being individual, it cannot be stated in a formula. It is secreted in the qualities of men. During his illness I had the rare opportunity of many talks with Senator Vandenberg on this subject, wholly divorced from any specific task. For many years I had observed him and worked with him. But these talks were contemplative. We reviewed our experience and tried to draw conclusions from it.

## This Vast External Realm

What then are the qualities in men and the posture of circumstances which make for this creative process when policy is moved forward to a new phase? On the committee's side what is needed is a chairman or senior minority member who is widely respected and trusted in his own party. Such a man usually stands well with the opposition also. He must be able to think vigorously about new problems, though he need not have an original cast of mind. His great function is to bring suggestions within the realm of the possible, to use method as a means of molding a proposal to make it politically feasible. He will, of course, be a politician. He will protect the interests of his party, and perhaps of himself, so that what he becomes convinced is in the national interest is not done so as to injure his party or aggrandize its opponent. But he will not be tricky. What he requires as a condition of support will be frankly stated. He will keep in touch with his colleagues, particularly his own party colleagues, and have a pretty sound idea that what he agrees to back will have the needed support when the time for voting comes.

On the executive side what is needed is a man who can speak for the Administration because he knows it and is trusted by it. He, too, must keep in touch, be frank and not tricky, and must pursue the main objective without being deflected by the non-essential. These two men must have confidence in one another.

An example of this sort of collaboration occurred in 1948 between Senator Vandenberg, then Chairman of the Foreign Relations Committee, and Mr. Robert

Lovett, Under Secretary of State, which resulted in the Vandenberg Resolution, the precursor of the North Atlantic Treaty. Senator Vandenberg's position was unique. He was Chairman of the Committee; by understanding with Senator Taft he was given the lead on the Republican side in foreign affairs while Senator Taft had it in domestic affairs. His influence in both parties was immense. He was a master of maneuver and a superb advocate. He and Mr. Lovett trusted and liked one another. Mr. Lovett could and did efface himself from the public eye. His ability matched the Senator's. He had at his fingertips the facts and needs of the situation, the desired policy. This work together produced what neither could have accomplished separately.

Examples of similar work on a much broader base were the meetings which Mr. Hull held in 1944 with three separate groups from Congress in which were discussed drafts of the United Nations Charter prior to the Dumbarton Oaks Conference. Mr. Hull has described these fully in his "Memoirs."

The Secretary met first on four occasions with eight members of the Senate Foreign Relations Committee. That Committee was then organized with a view to having on it leaders of Senatorial opinion. That it had is seen by the composition of the group—Senators Connally, Barkley, George, Gillette, Vandenberg, La Follette, White, and Austin. But other Senators were interested in the Charter, too, and to draw them in without questioning the prerogative of the committee the Secretary held a separate consultation with what was then known as the 2B2H group—Senators Ball, Burton, Hatch, and Hill. Since the House Committee on Foreign Affairs did not then or normally include the party leaders in the House, the group invited to meet with the Secretary consisted of the Speaker and Majority Leader, Mr. Rayburn and Mr. McCormack; the Minority Leader, Mr. Martin; the Chairman and ranking minority member of the Committee, Messrs. Bloom and Eaton; and Representatives Ramspeck and Arends. The Secretary also used his great influence, in the quiet way of which he was a master, to induce the national conventions of both parties to adopt planks favoring an international organization to keep the peace. This whole effort was outstandingly successful —a classic example of persuasion through participation by a man who thoroughly understood congressional processes.

If these occasions of real accomplishment in cooperation are rare, they would be even more rare were it not for the far larger number of meetings—which are also the "oil of government," preventing grievances from going unaired, preserving *amour propre*, giving a sense of participation, and an opportunity to exercise authority over detail.

It is often said that the executive must "get along" with Congress and particularly with the Senate. If this means that concessions of policy must be made in the interest of outward affability, I do not agree. Personal relations will for the most part be courteous and friendly, as one would expect between gentlemen. But no one knows better than politicians and lawyers that men can battle most bitterly in the arena over important differences and yet maintain amicable personal relations and cooperate on other matters. The Eightieth Congress, with which President Truman had his fiercest battles, worked admirably in foreign affairs; and many of those who demanded the dismissal of the Secretary of State in 1950–52 joined in passing all the major legislation he laid before the Congress, including the Japanese and German treaties on the very eve of the campaign of 1952. Mutual respect is more important than affability.

We return always, I think, to a central truth. The relations between the executive and legislative branches of our government were not designed to be restful. We must not be disturbed and think that things have gone amiss when power striking against power, and being restrained, produces sparks. Congress has, for instance, always wished to inquire into the internal process by which a particular executive decision was reached; what employees had to do with it; what advice each gave. The desire is natural, but to indulge it would destroy the administrative process and organization. If an employee is to do his unintimidated best, he must be shielded from the unequal struggle with a congressional investigation. The responsibility must be borne by those political officers upon whom it properly rests—the Secretary and his chief assistants, appointed by and with the advice and consent of the Senate. I think the Congress understands the justice and necessity for a firm attitude here to preserve the integrity of the executive branch, and though a refusal of such requests often produces momentary irritation, the issue is rarely pressed.

Secretary Stimson believed strongly in the desirability of a question period in the House and Senate on the British model, during which Cabinet officers would appear on the floor and respond to questions submitted in advance. He was not alone in this. At the beginning of this government the practice was common. In July 1789 the Secretary of Foreign Affairs, Mr. Jefferson, "attended, agreeably to order, and made the necessary explanations." The Secretary of War, General Knox, appeared in August of the same year, twice before the House, and with President Washington, twice before the Senate. The President was displeased with his reception and did not return. The Act of September 2, 1789, creating the Treasury Department provided (as the law still does) that the Secretary was "to make report, and give information to either branch of the legislature, in person or in writing (as he may be required), respecting all matters referred to him by the Senate or House of Representatives, or which shall appertain to his office." The House discussed in 1790 whether Secretary Hamilton should make his report on the public credit in person or in writing and decided on the latter only because of the mass of detail involved. Mr. Justice Story was a strong advocate of the right and duty of cabinet officers to appear on the floor both to answer questions and to participate in debate. In 1864 a select committee of the House (vigorously supported by James A. Garfield) and in 1881 a select committee of the Senate (on which James G. Blaine served) recommended the right to the floor of both Houses for cabinet officers both to answer questions and to participate in debate. In 1912 President Taft in a message to Congress of December 19 made the same recommendation.

The Pendleton Committee of 1881 concisely sums up the argument for its view: "This system will require the selection of the strongest men to be heads of departments, and will require them to be well equipped with the knowledge of their offices. It will also require the strongest men to be the leaders of Congress and participate in debate. It will bring these strong men in contact, perhaps into conflict, to advance the public weal, and thus stimulate their abilities and their efforts, and will thus assuredly result to the good of the country."

At one time I thought this proposal had more merit than I do now. It seems to me an ill-suited graft upon the committee system, on the one hand, and the presidential system, on the other. A Secretary who developed a capacity for congressional debate might well be in trouble on two sides. On one side he would be rivaling and diminishing the position of the chairman of the committee concerned. Out of this much trouble could grow. The other hazard, as Mr. Laski pointed out in *The American Presidency,* would be the development by Cabinet officers of a status and interests independent of the President, reminiscent of Stanton's with President Johnson, another impediment in the way of unified administrative policy. I doubt, too, the assumption in the Pendleton report and in Mr. Justice

Story's argument that the "strongest" men, "statesmen of high public character" best qualified for the administration of policy, are necessarily those best qualified for debate in Congress. Sometimes men are gifted in both endeavors; but, as I have observed government for a good many years, it is as often, perhaps more often, not the case. It is interesting that the Confederate Constitution had a provision permitting cabinet officers to sit in the Congress upon invitation. But the invitation was never issued, for fear that to do so give the President too much power.

More important, perhaps, than considerations which must remain theoretical, is the fact that our chambers do not have the tradition of discipline in relevance which permits Mr. Speaker in the House of Commons to maintain strict control over the question period. In May 1950, after a European conference, I had an experience of an informal congressional question period in an appearance before the members of both Houses in the auditorium of the Library of Congress. The questioning in this meeting seemed to bear out the misgivings I have expressed.

The architecture of our government is, I think, too set, practice has adapted it too well to our continental scope, to have it improved by additions or embellishments in the parliamentary style. The larger truth is that the two systems operate as *systems*—each with its general strength; each paying some price in weakness for the strength it has. To graft some special trait of the one onto the other, without regard either to the whole of the society it serves or to the whole legal and extra-legal framework into which it fits, will not produce better performance, but only a fracture, in the exercise of responsible power.

We have in this country been developing methods of our own by which, for instance, some members of the Congress can gain personal experience in foreign relations and in meeting and understanding the attitudes of foreign peoples and governments. The practice has grown up—and it is a good one—of having alternately two Senators and two Congressmen on the United States Delegation to the General Assembly of the United Nations. Subcommittees of the Senate and House Foreign Committees for geographical areas are kept closely in touch with developments in these areas. They often travel in these parts of the world when Congress is not in session. Indeed congressional travel is widespread and, for the most part, to the good. If sometimes a particular country seems to be subject to mass invasion, and if the inevitable press conference by the visitors rarely produces beneficial results, the price is not too heavy for the increase in understanding which comes with personal experience.

Today it is of new and pressing importance that the House have understanding of foreign affairs. The time has passed when the Senate monopolized the congressional function in this field, since it is the execution of policy, calling for legal authority, funds, and men, which is the ultimate test of success or failure. The importance of the House has grown and is growing, presenting new problems of giving information and a sense of participation to so large a membership. I venture to say that if it were possible to assess the factors which led to the erroneous Soviet judgment of our probable reaction to the invasion of South Korea, the defeat in the House of the Korean Aid Bill (H.R. 5330) on January 19, 1950, would bulk large. Would it seem likely in Moscow that a nation would come to the military assistance of another which its popular assembly had been unwilling to aid with funds?

In the years in which I was associated with it the House Committee on Foreign Affairs was a hard-working and understanding committee. Its security and its staff were excellent. The Committee did not carry the same weight in the House as did its counterpart in the Senate, so that unanimity became of special importance. A vociferous minority could make any result unpredictable. One of the masters of producing a unanimous committee without injury to the policy put forward was the late Congressman Bloom of New York, its Chairman for many years.

All that I have said about legislative-executive relations in the field of my experience can be summed up in a few sentences. It is not easy to conduct our foreign relations in the national interest with the limitations imposed by democratic political practices. A good deal of wear and tear will occur on the executive side, and it had best be liberally supplied with spare parts. Of all my principal assistants at the beginning of four years only one remained at the end. I found a rest not unwelcome myself.

# Legislative-Executive Relations

On the legislative side, a great danger, as in military operations, is to underestimate the problem. Legislators would do well to repeat to themselves: it is not as simple as we think. But the job can be done; and, if one would look for the "oil of government" which is of most help in the common task, it might be found in two quiet qualities, not much touted in politics, humility and disinterestedness.

# The Matter of
# Presidential Disability

President Eisenhower's unfortunate and recurrent illnesses have led to a good deal of discussion as to what should be done in case of the President's "Inability to discharge the powers and duties of the said office," in which event, the Constitution says, "the same shall devolve on the Vice President, and the Congress may by Law provide for the Case of . . . Inability . . . until the Disability be removed. . . ." The discussion has been revived by the recent understanding between the President and Vice President as to how each should act in the event of presidential inability to perform his duties.

The whole matter is, of course, a political one of some delicacy, in which the Constitution has laid down the main principles, leaving wide latitude in deter-

From the *Washington Evening Star*, March 17, 1958.

mining procedure. It would seem to call for a simple and common-sense solution, infringing as little as possible upon the prerogatives and powers of the President. But two deeply ingrained American traits impede this sort of a solution. One de Tocqueville noted a century and a quarter ago. "Scarcely any political question arises in the United States that is not resolved, sooner or later, into a judicial question," he wrote. So the debate, in this case, immediately becomes a legal one, and a highly legalistic one at that. Everyone becomes his own constitutional lawyer, especially columnists. This makes it hard for a guest columnist who happens to be a lawyer, but who believes that the problem is neither a legal one nor a very difficult one.

The other trait is our national addiction to complicating things. In this case we want to imagine every possible contingency and, by providing for all of them, produce a document as involved as a corporate mortgage or a marine insurance contract.

Discussion ought to begin, I suggest, by recalling that we are concerned with the occupant of the highest office in the land, the Chief Magistrate, in whom is vested the greatest powers legally placed in any Chief of State and Head of Government in the world. This should give rise to a decent reticence on the part of those who would interfere.

In the reign of Richard II the House of Lords vainly attempted to get from the judges an opinion on the Duke of York's claim to the throne. But the judges refused, saying this "mater was so high, and touched the Kyng's high estate and regalie, which is above the lawe and passed their lernyng; wherefore they durst not enter into any communication thereof, for it perteyned to the Lordes of the Kyng's blode . . . to meddle in such maters."

Now this was very sensible, and not only because it kept the judges' heads firmly attached to their shoulders. It is useful to recall this episode now and realize that the present matter is also "high" and touches the President's high estate and prerogatives which are above the reach of legislation, and, as a political matter, should be. It is also well to recall that the only "Lorde of the Kyng's blode" in this country is the Vice President, who, with the President, is the only official elected by the whole country, and elected for the very purpose of discharging "the powers and duties of said office" in case of the President's inability to do so. It would seem very proper then that he and the President alone are competent, as a matter of political wisdom and propriety, "to meddle in such maters."

The way in which the President has recently proposed to deal with his possible inability to discharge his duties seems to me sensible and politically desirable. He proposes, if he should be able to do so, to notify the Vice President of his temporary—if it should be such—inability, and ask him to discharge the Presidential duties. If he should be too ill to do this, the Vice President, taking such advice as he thought proper, would make the decision. When the President was again able to perform his duties, he would so notify the Vice President and resume their discharge.

# The Matter of Presidential Disability

This leaves the President in control whenever he is capable of exercising control.

The proposal seems to me politically and legally sound. On the legal side it would be highly desirable for the Congress by law to sanction this procedure; for there should be formal and public legal acts, such as publication in the *Federal Register,* for fixing the beginning and ending of this temporary transfer of power. But any attempt to have any group—judicial, legislative, executive, or mixed—empowered to determine the President's ability to perform his duties diminishes and endangers the office to an intolerable degree. We do not want any more delegations pulling back the bed-clothes of an ill President to see whether he can move his legs.

We must trust to the good sense of the man we have made Chief of State. If we are ever unfortunate enough to have a demented one, the ordinary processes of commitment should be adequate.

But, it has been said, once the Vice President performs the presidential duties, he cannot or should not step down. The legal argument seems to be that the Vice President must take the presidential oath, and once being sworn in, he cannot be sworn out. To this President Eisenhower replies:

> Why should he? . . . He has taken an oath as Vice President. . . .
>
> . . . The Constitution says the Vice President shall do certain things. It doesn't say he takes a new oath. It says under certain situations the Vice President does certain things, and when that situation is ended he

doesn't do them any more; and that is the way I read the Constitution.

That is the way I see it, too. If eminent men had not differed, I would find it hard to believe that there was an alternative to this simple and sensible view.

And why, as a matter of policy, should we want to interpret ourselves into a strait jacket? It is common practice with us, and in other countries, for the duties of even the highest offices to be performed temporarily by others. The President of the Senate yields his chair and gavel to the President *pro tempore* or any other Senator (Mr. Nixon has done this for about half of his term of office) and gets them back again without legal difficulties about oaths or practical problems of administration. So do the Speaker of the House, the Secretary of State, and others. Mr. Butler performed Prime Minister Eden's duties during his illness. Geroge IV acted as Regent during the long mental disability of his father.

Frankly, I cannot see the problem. But I can see the very serious problem which exists if we convince ourselves that the Vice President cannot act temporarily. It is not a theoretical harm but a real one, from which we have suffered in the past in, at least, three administrations. It is that no one performs the duties of the President or that they are performed anonymously by persons never selected by law to do so.

I have often wondered why we make this rather simple matter so difficult and in doing so distract our attention from the really hard problems.

# The President and the Secretary of State

## The Selection of a Secretary

On January 17, 1889, President-elect Benjamin Harrison wrote two letters to Mr. James G. Blaine. The first was short—only two sentences—and presented no difficulty. It offered Mr. Blaine "the position of Secretary of State," and asked for his early and favorable reply. The second letter was much more difficult, and between the first draft and the final letter lay revealing revision.

In the second letter, the President-elect wanted to say "some further and more familiar things." [1] His

From *The Secretary of State,* 1960, The American Assembly, Columbia University, ed. Don K. Price.

1. This and subsequent quotations from President Harrison, and relating to this correspondence, are taken from *Correspondence Between Harrison and Blaine,* ed. Albert T. Volwiler (Philadelphia: The American Philosophical Society, 1940).

instinct was right. Mr. Blaine was a distinguished and potent man—on the record to that date, more distinguished and potent than General Harrison. As one Blaine man put it in the very week these letters were written, "Blaine has been the leader of the party for years. H. is a mushroom." Blaine had been Speaker of the House of Representatives, Senator, Republican Presidential nominee, and for a few months under President Garfield, Secretary of State. More than anyone else, he was responsible for the nomination of Harrison. In short, Blaine was a power in the Party, perhaps *the* power, and his reputation in politics was not that of an idealist.

Harrison wanted to make three points: that Blaine should not expect the President to fill diplomatic posts with party hacks (Garfield's death and Arthur's administration were fresh memories); that certain outstanding questions with European countries—the Samoan controversy was one—should be solved and not exacerbated; and that Blaine should discipline his imperious nature in the interest of party harmony. This was no easy assignment, as the revisions show. Particularly interesting in the second paragraph is the presidential pen striking out the self-deprecating phrases of the Indiana lawyer—"the Indiana accident," as Mrs. Blaine called him.

> Your familiarity with the origin and progress of these
> differences [with the European countries], & ~~will enable~~
> would
> indeed with the whole history of our diplomacy ~~will~~ I
> am sure give you great advantage in dealing with them

# The President and the Secretary of State

& ~~will compensate for my lack of study & experience in foreign~~
~~Diplomatic affairs. I am a conservative by nature, and all the more a lover of peace from having seen a little~~
feel sure
~~of war. But~~ If in my ^ ~~strong & deliberate conviction that you can as Secretary of State make a very large~~ be very conspicuously useful to the country. ~~As to I am strongly~~
general
~~impressed with the thought that~~ I have another ^ purpose and duty in which I am sure you will cooperate with the greatest cordiality. It is to preserve ~~the~~ harmony of in our party. ~~The conspicuous fidelity Nothing~~ The continuance of Republican control for a series of Presidential terms is I think essential to the right settlement of some very grave questions. I shall be very
promote dissentions
solicitous ~~to~~ avoid anything that would ~~divide or disrupt.~~ ^ ~~You have not allowed any provocation to~~ and
civil service
very desirous that the ~~public business~~ ^ shall be ~~so conducted~~
placed and conducted
~~ducted as to establish our party upon~~ ^ that high plane
recommend our party
which will ^ ~~the~~ to the confidence of all our people. ~~You have never allowed any provocation to lessen your zeal & effort as a Republican and I am sure your wide acquaintance with our public men will enable you to give me valuable suggestion and very efficient aid in preserving that happy unity which in the recent election brought us success I knew you will~~ This purpose is absolutely disassociated with any selfish thought or ~~purpose~~
proper
~~pose~~ ambition, ~~and~~ I will be quite as ready to make ^ con-

237

cessions as to ask others to do so. ~~I shall give to~~ Each
                                              will have
member of my official family <sub>∧</sub> my full confidence
       I
and <sub>∧</sub> shall expect his in return. ~~Mistrust~~ . . .

There is no reason to doubt that the offer and the
acceptance were both activated, as General Harrison
wrote that they should be, by "a spirit of the most
perfect cordiality and confidence." Perhaps "perfect"
is too strong a word, for there had been a past of which
both men were aware. In Mr. Blaine's best-seller,
*Twenty Years of Congress,* he had written at some
length of the relations between another President and
another Secretary of State, President Polk and Secretary Buchanan. Among his observations were these:
"Mr. Buchanan was an older man than Mr. Polk, was
superior to him intellectually, had seen a longer and
more varied public service, and enjoyed a higher personal standing throughout the century." And again,

> The timidity of Mr. Buchanan's nature made him
> the servant of the administration when, with boldness,
> he might have been its master. . . .
> Mr. Buchanan, therefore, held absolute control of
> the situation had he chosen to assert himself.

If these passages give us some insight into Mr. Blaine's
approach to the new relationship, President Harrison
has thrown an even clearer light upon his own. After
leaving the White House, he wrote in 1893 a private

memorandum of his relations with Blaine. Two portions of it are relevant here.

> Mr. Blaine['s] relation to the convention of 1888 was a singular one. He felt I do not doubt even then such fears as to his health, and such misgivings as to his ability to endure a campaign that at times he spoke strongly and sincerely in declination of the honor which his many friends were urging him to again accept. But that at other times he hoped his declination would not be taken too strictly and toyed with the old ambition is more than probable—especially in view of his course in 1892. . . .
>
> My letter offering the portfolio of State to Mr. Blaine and his answer accepting the offer show the terms upon which our official relations were opened. My purpose was to keep them upon the basis of perfect confidence and friendship—or failing in that to make it plainly appear that the fault was not mine.

Harrison's reference to "his course in 1892" was to the crashing denouement of their relation. The inauguration was hardly over when Blaine asked that his son and close confidant, Walker, be made First Assistant Secretary of State. The President understandably refused. "All first propositions are rejected," wrote Mrs. Blaine. "It is a most uncomfortable twist in the make-up of a man."

Relations between the two became increasingly formal. Blaine's bereavements and stroke in 1891 led to the transfer of his duties to the White House. Irritations grew. On June 4, 1892, when a divided Republican convention was considering the renomination of the President, Mr. Blaine sent to the White House a curt note of resignation. Within the hour the President as curtly accepted it. "Well," he said, "the crisis has come."

Twice in our lifetime Presidents have chosen to be Secretary of State men who believed that the higher office should have been theirs.

As Mr. Truman has told us in his *Memoirs:*

> With this [his] impressive record, I felt that Byrnes could make a further major contribution if he were to be appointed Secretary of State. But this was not all. There was still another consideration, though it was mostly personal.
>
> Byrnes had felt that by virtue of his record of service to the party and the country he had been the logical choice to be the running mate of Franklin Roosevelt in the 1944 election. In fact, he had asked me to nominate him and give him my support before that convention.
>
> As it turned out, Roosevelt and the convention willed otherwise, and Byrnes, undoubtedly, was deeply disappointed and hurt. I thought that my calling on him at this time might help balance things up.[2]

Here, as in the case of Wilson and Bryan thirty years before, the relationship did not work. In a still earlier instance—with the same factors involved—it did work; but only because the President was our most

2. Quoted by permission from *Memoirs by Harry S. Truman.* Copyright 1953 by Time Inc.

magnanimous and patient one, and because the Secretary of State had the good fortune and ability to see the light in time. This was the relation between President Lincoln and Secretary Seward.

Lincoln's unexpected victory in the Republican Convention of 1860 was Seward's unexpected loss. Seward was the pre-eminent Republican Senator, and Lincoln, in his estimate, an upstart. The general view, as Rhodes's *History* of the 1850–1877 period put it, was that the nomination was a case of "the sacrifice of commanding ability in favor of respectable mediocrity." Seward was the Republican spokesman in Congress during the short session intervening between the election and the inauguration. He became deeply involved in the frantic interim efforts to stave off collapse of the Union. "Once for all," he wrote Mrs. Seward, "I must gain time for the new Administration to organize and for the frenzy of passion to subside." And again: "The revolution grows apace. . . . I have assumed a sort of dictatorship for defense."

And yet later: "It seems to me that if I am absent but three days, this Administration, the Congress, and the District fall into consternation and despair. I am the only hopeful, calm, conciliatory person here." And then, "Mad men North and mad men South are working together to produce a dissolution of the Union. The Present Administration and the incoming one unite in developing upon me the responsibility of averting these disasters."

And then after the counting of the electoral vote on February 13, 1861:

"We have passed the 13th safely. I am at last out of direct responsibility. I have brought the ship off the sands and am ready to resign the helm into the hands of the captain the people have chosen."

Seward was not ready for anything of the sort. He confided to his New York colleague in the Senate that Lincoln actually wanted him for a Prime Minister, and to a European envoy, that "there is no difference between an elected president of the United States and an hereditary monarch. The latter is called to the throne through the accident of birth, the former through the chances which make his election possible. The actual direction of public affairs belongs to the leader of the ruling party. . . ." He even tried tentatively to force his own will in the matter of Cabinet appointments. "The President," he wrote his wife, "is determined that he will have a compound Cabinet. . . . I was at one time on the point of refusing—nay, I did refuse to hazard myself in the experiment. But a distracted country appeared before me and I withdrew from the position. . . . At all events I did not dare to . . . leave the country to chance."

Seward did his best to prevail. He was one of the Cabinet minority of two in favor of withdrawing from Fort Sumter when the President insistently polled his advisers anew after a majority had at first favored capitulation. He turned desperately to the hope of finding his own specific field of responsibility—foreign relations—a basis for saving the Union: the precipitation of external conflict to reunify the riven nation. This would be coupled with an idea he had been advocating ever since the December of the interregnum—a complete concession to the South on slavery.

What led to the climax was Seward's resolve to draw the issue with a set of policy recommendations entitled "Thoughts for the President's Consideration." These he took personally to the President. Dr. Temple tells the story:

> Seward's criticism of the President's delay was severe. He had said: "We are at the end of a month's administration and yet without a policy, domestic or foreign"; further delay would "bring scandal on the administration and danger upon the country." But it was his final proposal that was most astounding. He said: "Whatever policy we adopt, there must be energetic prosecution of it . . . it must be somebody's business to pursue it and direct it incessantly. Either the President must do it, and be all the while active at it, or devolve it on some member of his Cabinet. Once adopted, debates on it must end, and all agree and abide. It is not in my special province: but I neither seek to evade nor to assume responsibility."
>
> Seward's offer to assume control was not limited to the foreign policy, but applied, as he said, to matters not in his special province. His demand that debates must end when a policy was once decided upon was a reference to Lincoln's second request for opinions on Fort Sumter after five out of seven members of the Cabinet had once given their judgment that the fort should be evacuated. The proposal was a very blunt expression of Seward's belief, which, it must be admitted, was that of many public men of the day, that he and not Lincoln was to be the real head of the Administration. Lincoln's

reply was in few words of unmistakable meaning: "Upon your closing proposition . . . I remark that if this must be done, I must do it. When a general line of policy is adopted I apprehend there is no danger of its being changed without good reason, or continuing to be a subject of unnecessary debate; still, upon points arising in its progress I wish, and I suppose I am entitled to have, the advice of all the Cabinet." [3]

That was the end of Seward as putative Prime Minister—the end of the most ambitious scheme yet put forward for establishing a coadjutor for the President. Two months later Seward wrote his wife: "Executive skill and vigor are rare qualities. The President is the best of us; but he needs assiduous co-operation. But I have said too much already. Burn this, and believe that I am doing what man can do." [4]

Now for once he was right. This was what he was doing. He was settling down to the complex tasks of running the foreign office as the President's agent—and beginning that estimable record of public service which earned him distinction and gratitude enough to fill any life.

These experiences are worth pondering. If, as Justice Holmes has said, in the life of the law a page of history is worth a volume of logic, it seems likely that in what is called political science these pages of history

3. The various quotations above relating to the Seward episode are from Henry W. Temple's "William H. Seward," in *The American Secretaries of State,* ed. Samuel F. Bemis.
4. Quoted in Earl Conrad, *The Governor and His Lady* (New York: Putnam, 1960), p. 357.

# The President and the Secretary of State

may be worth as many volumes of theory. At least it gives us a fairly solid point from which to start our discussion of the desirable relations between the President and his senior Secretary.

That point might be put this way: it is highly desirable that from first to last both parties of the relationship understand which is the President. Without this mutual understanding a successful relationship is most unlikely.

This does not mean subserviency on the part of the Secretary. In a much more hazardous age Lord Burghley saw and did his duty of standing squarely up to the great Queen when her interests and those of the realm required it. Much else, as we shall see, should rest upon this cornerstone of the relationship, the recognition of primacy. It is enough here to mention two mutual obligations. One, of course, is the Secretary's duty to see that the President is kept fully and timely informed so that he may perform his constitutional duty of conducting the nation's foreign relations with all the freedom of decision which each situation permits. The correlative obligation is that the President should perform his function of decision so clearly, and support his decisions so strongly, that action may flow from them.

The other obligation, only a bit less important to the success of the relationship than recognizing who is President, though less often achieved, is recognizing who is Secretary of State. A President may, and will, listen to whom he wishes. But his relationship with the Secretary of State will not prosper if the latter is not accepted as his principal adviser and executive agent in foreign affairs, and the trusted confidant of all his thoughts and plans relating to them. We can all recall times when this has not been true. Such times have always called for makeshift arrangements, the cost of which has often been considerable.

So far one can be dogmatic with some confidence. But not much further. The relationship is essentially one of partnership; and here, of course, personalities, experience and training, political exigencies, the nature of the times—all determine what the senior partner seeks in a junior partner to complement him.

One afternoon toward the end of November, 1948, I stopped at Blair House at the President's request. The request was not unusual, as I was at that time Vice Chairman of the first Hoover Commission, in the work of which the President was keenly interested. I anticipated nothing unusual. The President greeted me as I came into his minute study in the Blair-Lee House, and without further preliminary said that he wished me to become Secretary of State when his new term began in January. For reasons of sentiment he wanted General Marshall, then in the hospital after severe surgery, to stay in office until the anniversary of his taking office, January 21, 1949. This would coincide with the completion of the first Truman term.

Partly to collect my wits, partly to explore the President's mind, I asked that we discuss the matter for a while. Since some of the conversation which followed bears on the perplexing question of the selection of a Secretary of State, I shall summarize that part of it.

# The President and the Secretary of State

Some years of experience in the State Department, I said, made me one of the few persons invited to head it who knew the full extent of what he was asked to do. Moreover, I knew the tower of strength which General Marshall had been, having served under him. As I looked at the problems, I was appalled to measure my capacity beside them.

The President replied that without doubt there were people in the country more capable of being Secretary of State than I was, and more capable of being President than he was. The fact of the matter, however, was that he was the President and he wanted me to be Secretary of State. It seemed a waste of time to talk about that any further.

I made one more try for time. Several people, I said, mentioning them, clearly called for consideration. Might I, with propriety, ask whether the President had given thought to them? He most certainly had, and cheerfully told me exactly why each would be more useful to him in another private capacity. After a few minutes more of private talk, I was sent off to sleep on the problem and to answer in the morning.

To list all the qualities and qualifications which a President would do well to seek in a Secretary of State would be to belabor the obvious. It would also be silly, since in each instance specific men, and not abstractions, are involved. I remember a series of board meetings devoted to making a most important appointment upon which the members held strong and conflicting views. It was suggested that we first agree on the qualifications for the position before discussing individuals. I asked my neighbor what he thought of this logical procedure, to which he replied, "Nothing matters till we start to vote."

Enough has been said to suggest the two basic truths in this matter of the selection of a Secretary; one negative, the other positive. *First,* a President will be disappointed if he chooses as Secretary a man of greater political stature than himself, in the belief that the appointment will add to the power of his administration, or will placate a rival's resentment, or that the rival—to quote President Harrison again—will "do less harm inside than outside." *Second, a* President's best guide is a sense of confidence in his appointee and a belief that the man can help him more than others in dealing with the problems he sees ahead. In informing a President's judgment on this point, there are no rules. The experience of having worked together, where this has occurred, is invaluable.

## *The Nature of Foreign Relations*

The nature of an undertaking must obviously have a great bearing on the desirable relations between those who are directing it. Running a battleship is different from running a bank and calls for differences in the relations between the top men. Two factors make the nature of the problems of our foreign relations quite different from those existing, say, in agriculture, finance, or the administration of justice.

# The President and the Secretary of State

First of all, we are dealing with people and with geographical areas which are beyond our jurisdiction and control. Within our borders our government may command. Beyond them it cannot. In the second place, what is occurring in what the Supreme Court has called "this vast external realm" is so complex, so complicated, and so voluminous that we cannot currently comprehend it; nor, until too much time has elapsed, grasp its full significance. This is not wholly, or even principally, because of man-made impediments to knowledge—iron curtains, censorship, etc.—but because of the obscurity and complexity of the molecular changes which combine to bring about the growth or decay of power, will, and purpose in foreign lands. While it was reasonable to suppose that changes in the relative power of European states had occurred in the four or five decades before Sarajevo, not even the First World War wholly revealed how great they were. The facades of vanished power, including our own, still deceive us. Even yet our understanding of this changing world is far behind the fact.

This means that the basic problems of our foreign relations are those of understanding the true nature, dimensions, and immediacy of the problems which confront us from abroad and of putting in train the measures with which to meet them. These problems are particularly hard for Americans to keep in focus. Townsend Hoopes writes: "Our difficulty is that, as a nation of short-term pragmatists accustomed to dealing with the future only when it has become the present, we find it hard to regard future trends as serious realities. We have not achieved the capacity to treat as real and urgent—as demanding action today—problems which appear in critical dimension only at some future date. Yet failure to achieve this new habit of mind is likely to prove fatal." [5]

Years ago, when I was about to assume sobering responsibilities, an old lady expressed the short-term pragmatic view when she said to me, "Always remember that the future comes one day at a time." This was heartening and wise advice. At times one must live by this faith with thanksgiving. But, like most wise sayings, it is not the totality of wisdom. While it is true that the problems of the voyage come to the mariner day by day, it is essential to his success, and perhaps survival, that he know where he is going, keep on course, and also use all the knowledge at his disposal to learn what forces are building up around him and to prepare, as best he may, for what lies ahead.

Foreign policy is not a book of answers. Our foreign policies—for many are needed—should be interconnected courses of action adopted and followed to meet external conditions confronting us. The action of others beyond our borders can rarely be exactly predicted, and may take us by surprise. But these actions may be modified greatly in our interest if our courses of action have been founded on correct analyses of conditions and have been vigorously followed. Should we still be surprised by acts hostile to us, we can act more effec-

5. Quoted by permission from *The Yale Review*, Spring 1960. Copyright Yale University Press.

tively to counter them if our policies have given us the capability of doing so.

At the heart, therefore, of the conduct of our foreign relations, a task confided to the President, lies this primary task of understanding the forces at work abroad, and devising, adopting, and energetically following courses of action to affect or meet these forces. Important as other essential tasks may be, it is this one which should most color the relations between the two men principally involved with it, and hence the President's judgment in choosing his foreign Secretary.

One can see at a glance that if these two men are going to do their work properly they have got to spend a lot of time together, much of which may not be pleasant. The problems are frustrating. They are sure to provoke controversy in many quarters. Most of the desirable measures are distasteful to accept. All of the decisions are hard. So the Secretary of State has the makings of an unwelcome visitor. But for the President to delegate the functions of understanding and deciding is to delegate his office. The worst of all courses would be for the President to delegate the function of understanding to some super staff officer and retain the function of deciding, or apparently deciding, for himself.

So, to get the job done and to have the relationship successful needs solid mutual respect, based upon conviction by each that the other is wholly straightforward, loyal, and living up to his full obligation. It helps enormously to maintain mutual confidence if there is a strong admixture of affection between them; for in Washington they are working in an environment where some of the methods would have aroused the envy of the Borgias.

## *The Hierarchical Position of Secretary*

The reader will already begin to gather one bias of the writer which will run through this chapter: that the relationship between the President, our Chief of State and Head of Government, and his Secretary of State, his chief adviser and executive agent in the conduct of our foreign relations, is an intensely personal one. Insofar as this relationship is attenuated or institutionalized—or Parkinsonized—the task on which they should be jointly engaged suffers. We need to rediscover the individual in government, not submerge him. This does not mean that either man should act, as prototypes of both have done, independently of the rest of the government, or in the Secretary's case, independently of the Department of State.

The busy advocates of elaboration in organization are pressing in upon the relationship from both sides. On the President's side, the National Security Council already has a staff of its own. This staff must have some one to report to; but must not bother the President, whom it was supposed to help, since he cannot give the time if he is to be able to think. So—true to Parkinson's law—some of his functions are to be devolved upon two new officials, a First Secretary of Government (a sort of prime minister) and a General Manager of Government (a species of superior managing clerk.)[6]

The Secretary is thought to need relief too. One proposal would do this by incorporating the defects of Defense Department organization into the State Department. The Secretary, like the President, is to be relieved of duties so that he, too, can think. Below him his subordinates undergo an inflation of titles. The Secretary is to be elevated into the higher realms of pure policy, with a staff, to keep him from contaminating contact with action. He would preside over three or four service secretaries to whom the bureaucracy would report: A Secretary for External Affairs, who would do all the traveling (Vice President in Charge of Sales); a Foreign Minister, who would run the State Department (Vice President in Charge of Production); a Secretary of Public Affairs, who would head the United States Information Service (Vice President in Charge of Advertising); and a Secretary for International Development (Vice President in Charge of Exports).

The result of this reorganization would give the President and the Secretary plenty of time to think and talk, but not much to think or talk about. It will not be recommended in this paper. Here we shall

6. For a somewhat similar suggestion, see the statement by Governor Nelson A. Rockefeller before the Subcommittee on National Policy Machinery of the Senate Committee on Government Operations, July 1, 1960.

assume that the persons bearing the titles of President and Secretary of State exercise their familiar powers and perform their familiar functions.

From this point of view, what should be the position of the Secretary in the hierarchy of the President's advisers and executive agents? Obviously, it is going to be determined in large part by the character of the men involved. Secretaries Hughes, Stimson, and Marshall had within them a natural force which Secretaries Lansing and Colby could not equal. Secretary Hull was intimidated by President Roosevelt, who was, in turn, bored by the Secretary. It is idle to press men into types. But we can speculate on the position and influence which we could properly hope that ability, character, and luck would combine to confer upon the Secretary of State.

Protocol assigns to the Secretary the senior position in the Cabinet because his office and department were the first created. The nature of the times in which we live should assign him pre-eminent influence because of the paramount importance of foreign policy and the need that domestic and defense policy be shaped in aid of it.

To some this has meant that the Secretary of State should be elevated into a sort of prime minister, coordinating and directing other Cabinet officers under the President's authority and supervising eye. This will not work. No Cabinet officer can direct other Cabinet officers. Neither can any Presidential assistant, whatever his title; nor should he. In cases where the latter has, for a time, seemed to be doing this, power has become anonymous, and the President, for one reason or another, as *roi faineant*. There can be no more dangerous situation in a constitutional system such as ours, where the President exercises—or there are exercised in his name—vast powers affecting the very survival of the nation and people.

At this point it is essential to differentiate between the proper scope of the Secretary's interest and influence within the government and the proper scope of his legal authority. To give him legal authority over the Defense Department, for instance, as has been suggested, would further weaken and confuse the conduct of military affairs. Nevertheless, he has deep concern in a great variety of matters with which government must deal. He is not merely a department head whose jurisdiction is bounded by the diplomatic field. Foreign policy is the whole of national policy looked at from the point of view of the exigencies created by "the vast external realm" beyond our borders. It is not a "jurisdiction." It is an orientation, a point of view, a measurement of values—today, perhaps, the most important one for national survival. Obviously, our military capability to do or deter certain specific and varied things has an immense bearing on foreign policy. So does our economic capability, that of our friends and adversaries, and their relative growth or stagnation. Since internal fiscal and economic policies, public and private, affect both military and economic affairs, they, too, affect foreign policies or can affect them.

Of course, it can be argued—as, indeed, it has been argued, and successfully, in the past eight years—that —fiscal considerations are the paramount ones. When this point of view triumphs, fiscal and budgetary considerations will determine the rate of economic growth and fix the limits and direction of foreign policy. This situation is tolerated only when the dangers from abroad are given a low rating. In time of war or clearly recognizable national emergency, it is not tolerated for a moment. One of the ironies of the present is that its dangers appear to diminish in direct relation to our ignorance of them as a people.

When the security of the country demands that considerations of foreign policy shall dominate the more parochial interests of finance or of military strategy and tactics, the final decision and synthesis lie not in any of them, but in the Presidency.

To give the Secretary legal authority in these far-flung fields would be to usurp the Presidential office. But the best, even a good, operation of government requires that the Secretary be able to advise about the most important of these matters from the point of their incidence on our foreign problems and policies. It requires, too, that this advice be given great and respectful consideration. Neither of these requirements can be met unless the Secretary has the personal capacity and the necessary help to think more, and more deeply, than others about the nation's needs and interests, as a state among other states, in a world of change and movement and of unparalleled danger.

The President is the mode by which this can come to pass; and, the only mode. Unless the Secretary has the President's most intimate and abiding confidence and respect, he is only a diplomatic bureaucrat. He must not merely persuade the President but press him with all the means at his command to use the Presidential influence, authority, and where available, command to resolve national policy in accordance with the scale of values just mentioned.

At one point in the Korean War a difference arose between the State and Defense Departments on policy toward defecting Chinese prisoners. The Defense view was that the test of policy should be the military desirability of getting back as soon as possible our own men held prisoner. State insisted that the United States and the United Nations should not compromise in any way the position that prisoners defecting from the Communists would not be handed over to them. To hand them over would involve the widest consequences in Communist and non-Communist countries and to the integrity of the United States government.

The Secretary of State did not persuade the Defense Department to accept his view. He got the President to order them to do so. If it becomes clear that 90 per cent of the time the Secretary will get the President's backing, it becomes unnecessary to carry the majority of disputes to him. If, on the contrary, it is evident that the views of the Secretary of the Treasury will prevail, then fiscal and budgetary considerations will fix the limits and direction of foreign policy.

### The Multiple Nature of the Secretary's Function

Three aspects of the Secretary's function wherein his success or failure will be most immediately determined seem to me to have gone almost unrecognized. We may call these his corporate character, his judicial character, and his diplomatic (in the sense of representational) character within the government of the United States.

I have spoken of the "State Department" and of "it." In fact, of course, the work of the Department is performed by many thousands of trained, intelligent, and devoted men and women in all parts of the world and in Washington. Some Secretaries of State have carried on their work as though these people did not exist. On occasion they have been treated like clerks of whom all that was asked was "positive loyalty" to the administration in power, and that they be neither seen nor heard. This is a mistake. My own view has been expressed before:

> . . . Popular conceptions about government are in large part interesting folklore; and the instinct of the bureaucracy for self-preservation and the egotism of the chiefs [of Departments] perpetuate it. One of these concepts is that "policy" originates at the top and is passed down.
>
> To be sure, *great decisions* are, for the most part, made at the top, when they are not made by events. But, as for policy—the sum total of many decisions—it must be said, as it has been said of sovereignty, that its real sources are undiscoverable. One fact, however, is clear to anyone with experience in government: the springs of policy bubble up; they do not trickle down.
>
> When this upsurgence of information, ideas, and suggestions is vigorous, appreciated, and encouraged, strong,

imaginative, and effective policies are most apt to result. When the whole function of determining what is what, and what to do about it, is gathered into one hand, or into a small group at the top, the resulting action may or may not be strong, but it is likely to be ill-adapted to reality and self-defeating.

What has just been said underlines the judicial element in the function of headship and the great importance of interplay between head and staff at all stages in the development of decisions. By this I mean that the chief must from time to time familiarize himself with the whole record; he must consider opposing views, put forward as ably as possible. He must examine the proponents vigorously and convince them that he knows the record, is intolerant of superficiality or of favor-seeking, and not only welcomes but demands criticism.[7]

In other words, the individuals organized under the collective designation, Department of State, are not merely aids or subordinates of the Secretary of State. They are originators, as well as executors, of foreign policy. In the course of his meetings and discussions with them the Secretary can and should guide his colleagues in the Department into an understanding of the purposes and problems of national policy as they appear to the directors of government policy as a whole. The method, manner, and time of actions abroad can in a wide variety of situations be adjusted to a broader plan of campaign.

For converse reasons, as already stated, all the actions of government should harmonize with and sup-

7. *The New York Times,* October 11, 1969.

port—or, at least, not weaken—its foreign policy. To accomplish this, the President and some Cabinet officers must be kept continually aware of probable and possible developments looming in the outside world and of the courses which seem to be indicated. This is essential to wise national planning.

It is in this sense that the Secretary of State is, in some important part, an intermediary between two groups, both of which are in a proper sense beyond his control: the government as a whole, for obvious reasons; the State Department, because its duty is to report facts, honest opinion on them, and to make honest recommendations. When in the early 1950's the attempt was made to punish the honest reporting of unpleasant facts and unpopular opinions, the departmental and foreign services were preserved only by the almost indestructible nature of a bureaucracy. The French bureaucracy, for instance, survived the great revolution, two empires, and five republics with little change. The Secretary's role is one in which command is not an important function. It is one of guidance and influence.

This role can be successful only if his colleagues within and without the Department have complete confidence in his integrity and disinterestedness. Then only will the President be willing to accept and rely upon reports and recommendations which must nearly always be troublesome, if not worse. Similarly, if the men and women of the Department know that their work is respected and used in the most far-reaching decisions, they will give their best and cheerfully accept ultimate decisions which must weigh factors beyond their responsibility.

A good deal of the education of a Secretary who will accept it can come through the work with his colleagues which I have just described. These are not only diplomatic officers. There are also officers trained and working in fields which are not usually thought of as within the purview of a foreign office, although they are vital to foreign policy—economics, trade policy, finance, nuclear energy, etc. The Secretary needs their help and advice. From time to time the Budget Bureau wishes to abolish these positions, believing that adequate advice and help could be obtained from the Departments of the Treasury, Commerce, the Atomic Energy Commission, etc. This is quite untrue. The difficulty is like that which arises in translating foreign legal papers. The translator must know not merely the two languages, but the two legal systems. Otherwise he is worse than useless.

Beyond the scope of these non-diplomatic assistants, many problems which must concern the Secretary and his colleagues involve—and will increasingly involve—science and technology and judgments requiring knowledge in these fields. Within the government there are men who have this knowledge and, perhaps, could form these judgments. But these men are already overburdened with pressing tasks which are their primary concern and which, quite naturally and properly, may well impair their objectivity as advisers on some of the problems on which the Secretary may need help. Where help in dealing with these problems, and with what is called long-range thinking, may be sought is discussed in the last section of this chapter.

## The Secretary's Working Relations with the President

Here, again, everything depends on the temperament and character of the men involved. But one can note certain recurring circumstances. President-elect Harrison wrote, and then struck out, in his letter to Mr. Blaine a reference to "my lack of study and experience in foreign affairs." He was a perceptive and truthful man; but the presidential instinct prevailed. In 1960 an unusual number of the aspirants to the White House have had some exposure to foreign affairs through study and travel. This will doubtless fortify a conviction of competence in foreign affairs which soon comes to a President and to his personal staff, often outrunning the fact.

This is not peculiar to Presidents. To columnists, correspondents, legislators, some academicians, and most New York lawyers over forty, foreign affairs are an open book, though they often differ on the meaning of the text. Their opinions are available to the President directly, through the press, and through reports of various groups, more or less devoted to the study of our foreign relations. These opinions usually call for a change from conventional, unimaginative, and outmoded policies—i.e., those currently being followed—in favor of flexible, dynamic, and forward-looking policies, governed by faith and hope in the future rather than by fear and distrust.

From these groups comes a great deal of advice which reaches the President through the White House staff. To this staff foreign affairs present the ideal subject for a speech by the President. By "ideal" is meant a speech which will attract not merely national but worldwide attention and comment; a speech which will display "world leadership" on a "high level"; and which will not produce disagreement within the party, such as might come from a speech on tax revision or on the issues presented by school or farm problems. The State Department is apt to be terror-stricken by these suggestions, with very considerable justification. But to oppose is a losing gambit.

Since the Secretary cannot, and perhaps should not, stop these initiatives, he had better join them. And he must do it himself. No one down the line—least of all a speech writer—can control the White House composers gathered around the Cabinet table, with a draft of a foreign policy speech before them and the bit in their teeth. The Secretary, if he is wise, will join the fray himself, with his own draft, and try to guide and direct it. He can carry more weight than any of his associates, particularly in the final stages when the President himself, as I knew the procedure, joins the group and makes the final decisions.

It may seem absurd—and doubtless is—for a Secretary of State to be spending his time as a member of a Presidential speech-writing group.[8] But this is often where policy is made, regardless of where it is supposed to be made. The despised speech, often agreed to be made months beforehand without thought of subject, a nuisance to prepare and an annoyance to deliver, has often proved the vehicle for statements of far-reaching effect for good or ill. As both a junior and a senior official, I have fought this guerrilla warfare, sometimes to get things done which would otherwise be stopped, and sometimes to prevent others from doing the same thing. The Point Four proposal contained in the Inaugural Address of January 20, 1949—in which I was not involved—can be used to illustrate many points made here.

While on the subject of the White House staff, it is pertinent to mention a question which is often presented to all Cabinet officers: to what extent does a communication from the staff, or from the Executive Office of the President, represent a presidential order? The Executive Office is a congeries of agencies housed in that monument of late Victorian architecture adjoining and to the west of the White House—the old State, War, and Navy Building.

The most notorious of these, perhaps, is the Budget Bureau. Obviously its vast and pervasive intrusion into the business of diplomacy, conducted under the authority of the President, represents at most only his

8. My former colleagues tell me that I exaggerate my participation in presidential speech-writing. They are doubtless right. Messrs. Philip Jessup, Paul Nitze, Marshall Shulman, and others all did much of the work which I have described here.

most general decisions. Armed with these, a host of zealous, able, and, often, uninformed young men inquire, through hearings in which officials must "justify" their appropriation requests, into the innumerable policies and programs of the Department. The attempt is made to assign costs to various activities and to reduce the appropriation requested by striking out moneys thought to be representative of the cost of activities not adequately "justified." This rarely gets at a quite appropriate area of saving, which I shall not betray my old friends by disclosing. The importance of this budgetary process lies in the President's order that no executive agency may ask for more funds than are included for it in the President's budget. Therefore, as the process nears its conclusion, the Secretary, if he believes that some vital activity has been grossly handicapped, armed with the vigor of his outrage, goes to the President for redress. Rule by the Budget Bureau has often seemed to me aptly described as tyranny tempered by assassination. That of the House Committee on Appropriations is entirely untempered.

In a different form the personal staff in the White House can often pose the same question whether an order or request is what it purports to be. On one occasion a note from a member of the staff informed me that the President had learned that a certain foreign service officer was stationed in an African "hardship post" and wished him transferred to a more healthy spot. I took the note to my next meeting with the President. Before showing it to him, I said that I wanted to know whether he had, indeed, issued this instruction, in which case it would, of course, be obeyed. In doing so, I pointed out, other changes of personnel would become necessary and it might be desirable to refer the whole series of decisions to the White House, although they hardly seemed worthy of the President's time. He read the note, tore it up, and we went on to the next item.

Returning from this digression to the working relations between the Secretary and the President, there were times when I would see the President on business almost every day, and rarely less than four times a week. Every Monday and Thursday we met alone for a half an hour to an hour; or two other days in the Cabinet and in the National Security Council. Special meetings prepared him for foreign visitors, to deal with a variety of emergencies, great and small, to confer with groups of Senators and Congressmen, and so on. Finally, we talked frequently on the White House telephone.

The private meetings began by disposing of his and my agenda of specific matters, such as appointments, troubles (foreign and domestic), legislative goals and obstacles. The great utility and importance of these meetings lay in the opportunity for talk, talk in which I could learn from the President his thoughts of all sorts; what portended in the domestic field or in defense matters and their probable effects on foreign policy; how he was appraising the consequences of various actions of ours abroad; whether our conduct had or lacked congressional or popular support and what should be done. Then, again, these talks gave me an important opportunity to prepare him for developments which were foreseen by my colleagues and to discuss courses of action before crises burst upon us. In short, over the years these talks enabled us not only to keep one another informed but to see events and choices each from the other's point of view. This, I venture to suggest, can play a more effective part in developing a coherent national policy than the multiplication of staff and what is called "coordination."

President Truman, as his memoirs tell us, believed that he was not kept currently and adequately informed of Secretary Byrnes's negotiations when the latter was attending international conferences abroad. Having observed the consequences of this opinion on the President's part and the reporting procedures which General Marshall inaugurated, I determined to carry these procedures a bit further. The result worked well from all points of view, the President's, the Department's, and the delegation's.

Accompanying the delegation was a small secretariat whose sole duty, other than keeping me informed of the cables on developments elsewhere in the world, was the preparation and communication of reports of three types. Each evening a detailed descriptive account of the day's negotiations, prepared by a secretariat officer in attendance at the meeting, and checked by a senior officer, to which any significant memoranda of private discussions were added by my secretary, was sent to the Department with a copy for the President. This report contained the bulk of information on factual developments and chronology, and provided detail on the various national positions presented. It was widely analyzed in Washington by the various agencies concerned and was available as a basic reference for the President.

Also each day a condensed summary of the longer report was sent to the President through the Department. In this document we gave our opinions on the course which the negotiations were taking, the principal difficulties anticipated, and ways of meeting them. If instruction or guidance was needed on any point, it was asked for. Drafts of important statements, such as the Control of Armaments Proposals of 1951, were discussed in this section. The President, through the Department, and often the Department alone, commented and instructed (The Under Secretary, as General Marshall had insisted, was in fact as well as in title *Acting* Secretary.)

Finally, about twice a week, or more often when things moved swiftly, I sent a personal, "Eyes Only," message (which is not so restricted as it sounds) to the President, giving him my own opinions on how things were going, whether toward a successful conclusion as in the NATO meeting of February 1952 or toward failure, as in those of September and December 1951. I also sent in this form highly confidential information imparted to me, as for instance in May 1950, when Mr. Robert Schuman informed me of his coming proposals on the European Coal and Steel Company.

As a result of this systematic flow of information, the President was kept as familiar with what was going on as though he were present himself. He was always able to give, and frequently gave, direction, encouragement, and suggestions to the United States delegation. In consequence the delegation was assured that its course continuously had the full support of its government.

## The Central Task: To Recognize Emerging Problems in Time

In the section above on the nature of foreign affairs, I stressed the vast complexity of the myriad daily actions all over the globe which, like the combination of simple organisms into larger and more complex ones, form and shape the emerging future. The central task of a foreign office should be to understand what these forces are, to do what can be done to shape them favorably to our interests, and to prepare to deal with them.

This should be the task, but it is not. The principal effort goes into dealing with the overpowering present, the present, which, like the Mississippi in full flood, absorbs the whole energy and thought of those who man the levees.

Those who have never stood watch are impatient about this. "Act," they demand, "don't always *react*. Seize the initiative. The best defense is an offensive." And so the clichés go. Most of those who utter them are not expressing an idea, but rather an exasperation. But underneath the exasperation there is an idea—

and, what is more, a truth. It is a truth which makes mincemeat of most of the plans for reorganization of the conduct of foreign affairs.

The truth is that in foreign affairs manhours spent in thinking and planning on future action are by far the most profitable investment. The thundering present becomes so soon the unchangeable past that seizing it at any moment of its acceleration is as dangerous as mounting a train gathering speed. To change the metaphor, every bird-shooter knows that you must lead your bird and swing with its flight. This requires, in Mr. Hoopes's phrase already quoted, treating future trends as serious realities. To treat them in any way one has first to recognize them. Preoccupation with the so-called "machinery" for the execution of foreign policy misses this point. The true problem lies in determining the emerging future and the policy appropriate to it. It has been said of the late, unhappy Summit meeting that, once President Eisenhower had arrived in Paris, he dealt with the situation as well as one could. Undoubtedly so; but then it was too late for any action to have any effect. He could only emulate St. Sebastian by suffering the arrows of his martyrdom with dignity and Christian fortitude.

In an article in the *Bulletin of the Atomic Scientists* (March 1960), Mr. Roger Hilsman has gone to the heart of the matter:

> It is almost traditional in America to view foreign affairs as a problem in public administration. When our minds turn to the business of relating ourselves to the

outside world, we tend to think of reorganization, of rearranging the parts of the government. Yet all this organizational tinkering hardly seems rewarding. Many of our failures in foreign policy are probably not failures at all, but lack of power to shape the events we deplore. No nation is so strong that it can dictate the course of history, and much of what happens in the world is simply beyond our reach. What is more, one suspects that even our true failures in foreign policy would not have yielded to better organization. Good organization seems to imply efficiency in implementing policy, yet few of our true failures are attributable to bad administration in carrying policy out. Our true failures probably lie more often in failing to recognize emerging problems in time to evolve effective policies or in meeting big, bold, demanding problems with half measures, timorous and cramped.

It was the recognition of this source of our true failure which led General Marshall to establish the Policy Planning Staff when he became Secretary of State in January, 1947. This staff made a notable contribution for some years There were, however, inherent limitations upon its ability wholly to meet the need of recognizing and focusing attention on emerging problems. These can be laid only in part at the door of the Policy Planning Staff and its members.

The temptation to involve the staff in current operating problems has been too great on both sides. The staff members sorely want to have a hand in action rather than remain more remote from it, as planning, criticism, and analysis require. Then, too, the staff has often had on it some of the ablest men in the Department whom the high command cannot resist drafting, from time to time, for the more puzzling problems of the day.

Other limitations lie, partly, in the fact that the training and life of a foreign officer are not apt to produce men well fitted for the task we are discussing; and, partly, because the staff needed for the purpose should be larger and of more diversified professional training than the State Department will be permitted to, or probably could, obtain. The bureaucratic routine through which foreign service officers must go produces capable men, knowledgeable about specific parts of the world, and excellent diplomatic operators. But it makes men cautious rather than imaginative, and more guided by an intuitive hunch than by a judgment in which quantitative appraisal of voluminous data has played a part.

In the conception and development of the Marshall Plan the leading parts were, with few exceptions, played by men whose training and experience were broader than the State Department mill provided. The Fulbright educational exchange program was not of State Department origin; and the Point Four Program was vigorously opposed in the Department before its enunciation.

To peer into the yet unfolded future as it bears upon the relations of states in the latter half of this century is more likely to yield results if done by a group well staffed with scientists and technical people from many fields, including the military and economic, as well as with people experienced in all the world's areas and with its peoples. Such a group might discern in the detail of daily events patterns of emerging events, and be able to suggest courses of action to deal with them.

To accomplish this on a more elaborate scale than either the RAND organization or the Institute of Defense Analyses is now able to provide, Mr. Hilsman proposes, in the article cited above, a National Research Organization, with a congressional charter financed partly by an endowment, partly by contract work, and, perhaps on occasion by special appropriation. Its chief client would be the State Department, though other agencies in the Executive Branch and the Congress could contract for studies if they were willing to pay for them. The idea of an outside organization and of the contract relationship are to keep the group going independent of administration fashions in thought and to keep it efficient and competent.

Either Mr. Hilsman's proposed organization or RAND or the Institute of Defense Analyses could be of immense help to the State Department or the Secretary. Whether they would avail themselves of this help only experience can tell. Undoubtedly the apparent admission of insufficiency by acceptance of outside help would cause initial resistance. But this would be a mistaken view, and, if one is inclined to be hopeful, might be overcome in time. The very removal of this research and analysis from operations would give important reassurance against usurpation. The breadth of view, the infusion of military knowledge, which the military are too busy or too cautious or too circumscribed to give, and of technological knowledge and judgments, which are readily available elsewhere, would make this help invaluable, particularly to the Secretary, who would be alerted to developments not ordinarily uncovered by Departmental procedures.

One final observation upon the current plethora of reorganization plans may be appropriate. The passion for reorganizing the executive is a passion of Congress. Singularly unsuccessful in reorganizing itself—the last spectacular failure being the La Follette-Monroney effort in 1946—the Congress delights to turn its attention to the State Department which has the least defense against it. What it has done with foreign aid and propaganda, beginning with the Vandenberg-Brookings scheme of 1948, to date has both boxed the compass and demonstrated a strictly limited capacity to deal with the problem. It fairly raises the question of the extent to which the Executive should submit to the vagaries of Congress as to how it should conduct its consultations and the procedures for reaching its conclusions.

To be sure, the Congress obviously has power to prescribe the organization and procedures for expending the appropriations made for, say, the Marshall Plan; and the Comptroller General would disallow expenditures not made in accordance with law. But the Congress should not be encouraged to believe that it should determine the manner of Executive consultation and decision. Should the President believe that elaboration of the NSC organization, or other procedures provided by Congress, are of no use to him, he can and should disregard them and establish others more agreeable to him.

From the very beginning of our Federal government we have acted upon the constitutional theory that, especially in the field of foreign relations, the processes of consultation and decision among the highest officers of the Executive branch are essentially political processes within the responsibility and prerogative of the President. In this field the Legislative and Judicial branches have been admonished of the unwisdom of attempts to narrow the President's responsibility or scope of action. (See *United States v Curtiss-Wright Export Corp.*, 299 U.S. 304, 321.) This theory has happily accorded with political reality. Top policy councils work best when the President assumes responsibility for determining their form and procedures, for mastering their content, and for making the ultimate decisions. The Secretary of State can make his, and his department's, greatest contribution to wise and timely decision when he is accepted and used by the President as his chief adviser and executive agent in the field of foreign affairs. The President does not improve the conduct of business, peculiarly his, by inviting the Congress to organize it for him.

# The Eclipse of the State Department

## I

For over a decade it has been received as accepted truth in the highly charted political atmosphere of Washington that the role, power, and prestige of the Secretary and Department of State in the conduct of foreign affairs have steadily declined. Accompanying this decline, and accused of causing it, is said to have been an increasing part played by the President himself in this alluring, fashionable, and important activity, accentuated, perhaps, by the appearance in the White House of a court favorite—a modern Leicester, Essex, or Buckingham—served by over a hundred attendants and constantly advising the monarch on these

From *Foreign Affairs,* July 1971.

matters in the antechamber. *The New York Times,* in a series of articles published in January 1971, dates these developments from FDR's time, though adding that the trend was arrested "during the Truman and Eisenhower years [until] the death of John Foster Dulles in 1959."

Opinions have differed widely whether the eclipse noted is total or partial, radical and sinister, or within constitutional limits and historical precedents in relations between Presidents and the first State Secretary and department created by the first Congress. A great deal of the resulting debate has been based on wholly erroneous ideas of the nature and source of the national power to conduct foreign affairs, so we might do well to get this straight before going further.

## II

The Supreme Court has left no doubt that the Federal power over external affairs—unlike the power over internal affairs—is not the creature of the Constitution. The Union, it has pointed out, existed before the Constitution, and, with independence from Britain, the power to act "in the vast external realm" passed from the British Crown to the corporate unity, the United States of America. The Constitution strictly limited participation in the exercise of this power. "The President alone has the power to speak or listen as a representative of the nation. He *makes* treaties with the advice and consent of the Senate; but he alone negotiates. Into the field of negotiation the Senate cannot intrude; the Congress itself is powerless to invade it." The Court quotes the Senate Committee on Foreign Relations as reporting to the Senate on March 7, 1800: " '. . . the President is the constitutional representative of the United States with regard to foreign nations. He manages our concerns with foreign nations and must necessarily be most competent to determine when, how, and upon what subjects negotiation may be urged with the greatest prospect of success. For his conduct he is responsible to the Constitution. The committee consider this responsibility the surest pledge for the faithful discharge of his duty. They think the interference of the Senate in the direction of foreign negotiations calculated to diminish that responsibility and thereby to impair the best security for the national safety.' " [1] (What a committee that was!)

The Court notes also "that the first President refused to accede to a request to lay before the House of Representatives the instructions, correspondence, and documents relating to the negotiation of the Jay Treaty—a refusal the wisdom of which was recognized by the House itself and has never been doubted." I, myself, declined to furnish Senate committees investigating the relief of General MacArthur the names of department personnel participating in the preparation of a certain paper, made public by the General's office, as not compatible with the public interest. I did, how-

---

1. *United States* v. *Curtiss-Wright Corp.*, 299 U.S. 304, 315, *et seq.*

ever, appear myself and give such information as seemed pertinent to the committees' investigation.

Of course, in the daily conduct of business sensible people, whether in government, professional life, or business, do not insist upon a drily logical and extreme respect for the letter of their rights. Sometimes turning square corners is essential even though it produces irritation. In other situations, cooperation in a short-cut is in the public interest. When the bipartisan foreign policy flourished, I advised with the Chairman and senior minority member of the Senate Foreign Relations Committee—sensible men both—on the drafting of treaties and not only received many good ideas but in the course of it strongly predisposed the committee and the Senate to consent to the ratification of the treaties. Similar cooperation made possible much legislation to which Congress would not now agree. However, the Executive did not in the interest of "good relations" appease the Congress by permitting encroachments upon the President's prerogative to control exclusively the nation's foreign relations.

The first Congress created the office of Secretary of Foreign Affairs and the Department of Foreign Affairs to assist the President in performing his responsibilities. But it did not and could not delegate any of these or require him to accept assistance that he did not want or forgo any that he desired. The privileged position of the President and his advisers on foreign affairs is carried over into the field of manners, even though these are not what they were a century and three-quarters ago. "In the case of every department except the Department of State, the resolution [seeking information] *directs* the official to furnish the information. In the case of the State Department, dealing with foreign affairs, the President is *requested* to furnish the information 'if not incompatible with the public interest.' A statement that to furnish the information is not compatible with the public interest rarely, if ever, is questioned." [2]

A good deal more than a century ago, Alexis de Tocqueville observed that due to Americans' preoccupation with their written Constitution and the interpretation of it, every political question here sooner or later turned into a legal question. Neither the Constitution nor the law binds the President to monogamous cohabitation with the Secretary and Department of State in the conduct of foreign affairs. The relationship can have many advantages; it has often proved very inadequate and disappointing. We shall, I believe, find more revealing enlightenment about the current causes and consequences of its decline if we turn to the historical experience of another world power as well as to that of our own government.

## III

A move away from the local scene and local personalities may give us a more detached view. Sir William Hayter, former British Amsbassador in Moscow,

2. *United States* v. *Curtiss-Wright Corp., supra,* p. 321.

provides a start in his book, *Russia and the World*.[3]
In Moscow, as in Washington, the foreign office occu-
pies a large building housing the usual panoply for
conducting foreign relations. But decisions are not
made there or by that staff They are made in the
Politburo, the supreme executive authority of the
Communist Party, which controls all agencies of the
Soviet state. The Foreign Minister, Mr. Gromyko, is
not a member of the Politburo. Its head is Mr. Brezhnev, General Secretary of the Party, aided—if he needs
aid—by Mr. Kosygin, Chairman of the Council of Ministers.

The Politburo staff parallels the organization of the
foreign office (and other government departments as
well). Mr. Gromyko is also supervised by the KGB,
an even more jurisdictionally powerful counterpart of
Mr. J. Edgar Hoover's FBI, and his finances are controlled by an even more restraining hand than that of
Congressman John Rooney of Brooklyn.

With the Russians, the multiplicity of supervision is
carried into the field also, which explains why their
embassy staffs are so large and the hierarchy in them
so mysterious. More often than not the Ambassador
has little or no control over most of his staff and often
knows little of what is going on or what decisions are
being made. With us the situation in the field is better
than it was during World War II, as anyone knows
who lived in Old State through that anguishing period. Poor Mr. Hull's life was one long battle with

3. Sir William Hayter, *Russia and the World: A Study in Soviet
Foreign Policy* (New York: Taplinger, 1970).

the bureaucracies of other agencies—the military, Lend Lease, Economic Warfare, Treasury, War Shipping, Relief, Agriculture, and so on. He won all the linguistics of decisions and lost all the substance. What little order came out of it all was produced by Harry Hopkins at the White House, regarded by Mr. Hull as his mortal enemy. We envied the British Foreign Office for what seemed to be their effortless superiority.

When the Bolsheviks took over in Russia at the end of 1917 and began to sort things out, they had to create a system of party and state from their necessities. Few, if any, of the faithful knew much about the methods of foreign relations, or the possibilities, though more of the dangers, to be expected from the bourgeois states. What lay at hand was the wreck of the Tsarist diplomatic system. Full of suspicion, and from their training expecting to use and meet a diplomacy of deceit, they began the work of devising party apparatus to direct, to watch, and to police the work of a distrusted state organization. The resulting machine was clumsy, inefficient, and as fantastic as a Rube Goldberg cartoon; but after a fashion it worked.

## IV

At about the same time Lenin was having trouble with his foreign office—or, perhaps, a bit earlier—President Wilson was having trouble with his. For nearly seventy years after Secretary Seward's time the De-

partment did not have much to do. The correspondence between President Benjamin Harrison and Secretary James G. Blaine (published by the American
Philosophical Society) bears fascinating witness to
that. Although they wrote one another nearly every
day, their most important task was to draft and negotiate the Bering Sea Treaty protecting seals. At length
Secretary Blaine, believing that during his illness the
President had learned to get along without him, resigned in a huff. Not long afterward, on April 24, 1898,
after the U.S.S. *Maine* had been blown up in Havana
harbor and war declared against Spain, Secretary of
the Navy Long and President McKinley telegraphed to
Commodore George Dewey at Hong Kong directing
him to proceed to the Philippines and capture or destroy the Spanish fleet. Neither of them thought it
important to inform, much less consult, Secretary of
State, later Mr. Justice, William R. Day. Thus began
three-quarters of a century of American involvement in
the western Pacific.

Perhaps the clearest evidence of the fragility of the
Secretary of State's position occurred at the turn of the
century, as the infancy of American foreign policy was
ending. When Theodore Roosevelt succeeded William
McKinley in the White House, the Secretary of State,
John Hay, commanded immense prestige without,
however, much real basis for it. (Fifty years or so ago
I asked Justice Holmes what he thought of John Hay.
He replied that Hay's chief importance to him was to
give a line on Henry Adams.) Secretary Hay soon

reported that, while President McKinley would often see him on business only once a month, President Roosevelt would send for him every day. He soon discovered that a vigorous new force had taken over direction of American foreign affairs. During the Venezuelan crisis the President threatened the German Ambassador with the use of American sea power to block German occupation of Venezuelan territory. Not long afterward a by-no-means fortuitous revolution in Colombia created out of that country Panama and out of the latter the Canal Zone  No doubt remained that the conduct of affairs had passed from the hands of Secretary Hay, "the statesman of the Golden Rule," to President Roosevelt, who carried a big stick and did not always speak softly.

The formal "coming out" of the United States into international society did not take place until the unsuspected eruption of the First World War upon a basically nineteenth-century world and a wholly unprepared administration. The President had appointed as his Secretary of State the three-time loser for the presidency who had swung the Baltimore convention from Champ Clark to Professor and Governor Woodrow Wilson of New Jersey. The only contribution of Secretary Bryan to the subject matter of his new post was the negotiation of thirty-one treaties for the impartial arbitration of international disputes, very few of which were ever invoked. His principal contribution to the President's program was in the domestic field, helping importantly in getting through Congress the

# The Eclipse of the State Department

President's anti-monopoly legislation, known as the New Freedom.

With the outbreak of war in Europe, trouble soon followed in Washington between the President and his Secretary of State. Mr. Bryan reluctantly signed the President's first note to Germany protesting against the sinking of the *Lusitania;* but he balked at the second and tougher one and resigned his office. The President appointed to succeed him Robert Lansing of Watertown, New York, who had been serving for the preceding year as Counselor of the Department of State, after prior experience as counsel for the United States before various international tribunals. It soon became apparent that Mr. Wilson, having discovered and taken over the management of foreign affairs, was not prepared to release a scintilla of his authority. He was content to rely upon his own typewriter and the reports of his unofficial ambassador-at-large and collaborator, Colonel Edward M. House of Texas. Nothing escaped him. He could even write to Mr. Herbert Hoover calling attention to the words "our allies," appearing on posters of the Food Administration. "I would be very much obliged if you would issue instructions that 'Our Associates in the War' is to be substituted . . . because we have no allies. . . ."

When the time came to form the American delegation to the peace conference in Paris, Secretary Lansing advised the President not to go. Colonel House first gave contrary advice but changed it after consultations with Americans, French, and British in Paris.

The President resisted these counsels, which "upset every plan we had made." "I infer," he cabled Colonel House, "that the French and British leaders desire to exclude me from the conference for fear I might there lead the weaker nations against them." He decided to go and went. The outcome was a tripartite organization—the President with his secretaries, his wife, and his physician, Dr. Grayson; the delegation, all capable men but without influence with the Senate, which would have to ratify the treaty, and the delegation's staff; and Colonel House with a large and generally able group, known as "The Inquiry," but again without helpful political influence. As the weeks wore on, rivalry between the groups became hostility, increasing the burden upon a tired and harassed President. The result was organized confusion on a high intellectual level. In the sad years that followed the President's stroke, the defeat in the Senate of the treaty and the Covenant of the League of Nations, and the collapse of all his hopes, President Wilson broke with Colonel House, discharged Secretary Lansing, and left the State Department a shambles.

In the interwar years the management of our foreign policy was, for the most part, not divided; neither was it successful. Secretary Hughes, whose great abilities were not so clear in the State Department as they were later on the Supreme Court, is remembered chiefly for the Limitation of Arms and Pacific Treaties, the work of the Washington Conference of 1921. He failed utterly in efforts to save something in the Senate from the wreck of Versailles; and rejected all efforts of

# The Eclipse of the State Department

M. Chicherin to open some sort of relations, economic or political, with the Soviet Union, thus beginning the long boycott of that power. The Washington treaties limited naval construction, demilitarized certain islands in the Pacific (principally American-held) and relied on admirable principles intended to restore and maintain the political and territorial integrity of China. Their results, enhanced by American failure to build up to the naval limitations of the treaties and by Japanese failure to respect the provisions regarding China, made Japan the predominant power in the western Pacific.

This loss of real power was met by Mr Hughes's successor with a moral equivalent. There was already an established movement in this country, led by respectable people, for the outlawry of war, a sort of exorcising of evil spirits by moral incantation. The Foreign Minister of France, M. Aristide Briand, proposed to Secretary Frank Kellogg a treaty to this effect. The consciences of Americans had long suffered from the rejection of the Covenant of the League and the fatal repudiation of President Wilson. The outlawry of war seemed to offer "a full, perfect, and sufficient sacrifice, oblation, and satisfaction for the sins" of the irreconcilables and isolationists. It was also simple and painless. In Article I the parties "solemnly" condemned war as the solution of international controversies and renounced it as an instrument of national policy. In Article II they agreed that solution of disputes should "never be sought except by peaceful means." That was all, a covenant without means of enforcement. On July 24, 1929, with the adherence of forty-five nations, the treaty was formally proclaimd in effect.

The effect, however, was negligible. Within two years the Japanese had invaded Manchuria; the Italians, not long thereafter, Ethiopia; and the Germans and Italians, Spain. But none of these means of national policy had been called war. At the end of a decade the treaty had passed into such total oblivion that the fig leaf of verbiage was disgarded and the nations moved brazenly into World War II.

A free hand for the Secretary of State had not brought much improvement in resulting policy.

When President Roosevelt took office on March 4, 1933, he found as part of his inheritance a foreign office that he distrusted, if not as much as the Bolsheviks had distrusted theirs, at least rather more than he distrusted the rest of the governmental establishment. To use a phrase of his own, it was deep "in the horse and buggy age." Secretary Hull was no man to pull it out. His bitterness grew with his estrangement from the President until he found himself, in his own words, "relied upon in public and ignored in private." This was not lessened when the only interest the President took in foreign affairs during his first two terms was in the good neighbors of Latin America. There he looked for help not to Mr. Hull but to his subordinate, Sumner Welles, the President's protégé and former ward.

After nearly two terms in office, world war burst upon a President unprepared intellectually and mili-

# The Eclipse of the State Department

tarily. He and his Secretary of State responded, at first, with conceptions and phrases gleaned from General Washington's Farewell Address, President Wilson's Fourteen Points, and the program of the congressional interwar isolationists. These included non-involvement in European quarrels, quarantining dictators, preserving the peace (but by means short of war)—a jumble of confused clichés suggestive of our current response to troubles in the eastern Mediterranean, so much a product of our own creation. President Roosevelt's later course from bewildered observer to active belligerent owed far less to his own design than to the folly of our enemies. Surely the suicidal Japanese attack on Pearl Harbor, rather than, for instance, subversion in the Dutch East Indies, was one of the supreme errors of history. The German declaration of war against the United States, after four days of deliberation, long enough to have enabled Hitler to have seen the advantages to him in abandoning his ally, ranks as a fitting companion-piece.

The later formulation and conduct of war policy, controlled directly by the President with little assistance from the State Department, owed much to Harry Hopkins, who moved into the White House to be constantly at the side of his chief. In him and his work we can see the embryo of the Presidential Assistant for National Security Affairs of today. Ill and not tireless but fanatically devoted and diligent, he labored far beyond the limits of his strength until the effort killed him. The country owes him a vast debt of gratitude never adequately acknowledged.

# This Vast External Realm

In spite of Harry Hopkins' preeminence in the White House, he in no way interfered with or hampered the work in the State Department on the charter and the treaty of the United Nations. However one may appraise this accomplishment—and my own evaluation is not favorable—it was entirely due to Mr. Hull's long preparatory work with the Senate, the advice of his assistant, Leo Pasvolsky, and the management of the Dumbarton Oaks initial conferences and the final one at San Francisco, by Under Secretary, later Secretary, Edward R. Stettinius.

## V

The postwar State Department was created in President Truman's first term by General Marshall, whose military experience was of great help in getting rid of the horse and buggy and designing a functional chassis for fast-moving and heavy loads. Lines of command were clarified and the Under Secretary made chief of staff; line duties separated from staff duties; supervision was made effective through the Central Secretariat; planning—looking around, ahead and behind—confided to a competent staff; research and intelligence centralized. Equally important, the beneficent passage of time and rules of retirement made possible the renovation of personnel from the great numbers of able people brought into government by the war and selected by men who knew what qualities they wanted and who had them.

# The Eclipse of the State Department

Furthermore, General Marshall had the President's complete confidence, kept him fully informed of what was brewing, and carried back directions to officers concerned. Confluence of ideas was constant. Decisions on courses of action and reaction blended professional and informed advice and political judgment sound enough to provide policy through the next administration and beyond.

Marshall policies survived, but the Marshall State Department did not. Senator Joseph McCarthy, abetted by men who should have known better, led a crew bent on destruction; and Secretary Dulles offered no defense. The sack and massacre of the Department occurred, like Cromwell's at Drogheda and Wexford, after the assault had succeeded and, perhaps, for the same reason, to warn opponents against prolonging hopeless resistance. Many survivors were dismissed or sought more congenial employment. Friends have told me that, before accepting the post of Secretary, Dulles hesitated in favor of a room in the White House and the historical role of personal and private adviser to the President on foreign affairs. In the only conversation I had with him after he was designated as my successor, he said that he would save himself for policy decision and not spend the time I had done on personnel and organizational matters. I thought, but did not say, that he might find that these matters constituted much of the nine-tenths of the policy iceberg that lay below the surface.

By the time President Kennedy succeeded in 1961, successive purges in search of what Mr. Dulles called "positive loyalty" had left more form than substance in the Marshall organization and led the new President to doubt how positive its loyalty might be to him. Moreover, he had been indoctrinated—so it was said—by that gay savant, Richard Neustadt—now of the Kennedy School of Government at Harvard—in the belief that no professional departmental staff could be trusted to be as concerned as would be a personal White House one with the political effects upon the President of foreign policy (as well as other) decisions. Thus, once more, two factors—distrust of an existing organization and desire for a more personally controlled instrument—combined in Washington, as they had in Moscow, to create an inner and private Politburo to control and supervise a foreign office, whose new head the President hardly knew at all.

President Kennedy, however, went further and made his brother Attorney General. When he told me of this intention in the December before his inauguration, I advised against it on the obvious ground of his opening himself to charges of nepotism. He replied sadly that, while he knew many people who could and did help him to become President, he knew few who could help him act as President. He felt the need of a trusted intimate near him with whom he could talk without reserve. It very soon developed that the attraction of foreign affairs to anyone with easy access to the President proved irresistible to the Attorney General. He readily became another member of the controlling Politburo.

# The Eclipse of the State Department

## VI

The new organization, with staffs of size and competence, has now survived a decade of political life and
constant criticism. At its head Messrs. McGeorge
Bundy, Walt Rostow, and Henry Kissinger, all men of
outstanding ability, have served successively, to the an-
nounced satisfaction of their presidential chiefs. What
emotions they stirred in the breasts of their colleagues
at the State Department we must wait on future
memoirs to learn. Meanwhile, we can imagine that
there has been strain.

Debate is warming up over the issues whether the
present system has come to stay and whether it is, on
the whole, beneficial or harmful to the conduct of our
foreign relations. Many participating in this debate
have special interests, such as maintaining a position in
the process or prying a way into it; many base their
arguments on erroneous law or history; many are
moved by sentimental attachments, many by personalities. It is possible, however, that a few conclusions may
be pulled out of this devil's cauldron of debate.

Have present practices come to stay? Ten years of
life and the endorsement of three Presidents to whom
is confided the conduct of foreign relations would seem
to warrant long odds on continued life-expectancy. To
be sure, the resultant dual organization for dealing
with foreign nations is made to look something of a

monster and a clumsy one. But, as Justice Brandeis said of the separation of powers, it was not designed to promote efficiency; and the organization of the Pentagon, for instance, suggests the work of a madman with a sense of humor, a knowledge of history, and a lively civilian fear of a too-efficient military organization, like the old German General Staff. Moreover, the present arrangement, to some extent, has been in effect for most of the time in this century when the United States has had a foreign policy worthy of the name. We are apt to consider normal practice what we have been used to. It should not take much reflection to convince one that both President Truman's attitude toward the conduct of foreign affairs and his relationship with two of his Secretaries of State were by no means usual or to be expected as a matter of course. Surely it will be seldom that a President will find in the same man all the help he will want in deciding what to do regarding the external realm and in doing it. The point is that it will not be impossible, but that it will be often very difficult and incompatible with the temperament of Presidents like the last three.

He will want knowledge of diplomatic method and diplomatic history, greater familiarity with affairs around the world than membership in the Council on Foreign Relations will provide, public prestige (or acceptance) and negotiating capacity, the ability to use and direct a large government organization, not at all the same thing as heading a large manufacturing company, as Secretary of Defense Wilson (Engine Charlie) had already demonstrated. As one goes on adding desired capacities and experience, one must realize how seldom an adviser at the elbow and a minister of foreign affairs can be fitted into one human body. A clinching difficulty lies in the need that the assistant in the antechamber stay there—Secretary Byrnes records that one half his time in office was spent away from Washington. Much time has been wasted drawing organization charts to fit both functions into the Department of State. A presidential instinct to put the function where he needs and wants it seems more sound than forcing it into a procrustean organization chart.

Some participants in the debate appear to believe that the present arrangement must lead to a death struggle between the Secretary of State and the adviser in the White House. How can the former speak effectively to representatives of foreign powers, it is asked, when there is a rival in the White House? There is always a figure in the White House more important than the Secretary of State—the President—and often he does his own talking, sometimes to the embarrassment of a lot of people. A special adviser is most unwise to do any talking. A Secretary of State can always speak effectively if he speaks for the President, knows what he is talking about, and is telling the truth. Mr. Gromyko, despite defects in his power, is listened to when he meets these requirements, which he did not do when he talked with President Kennedy at the time of the Cuban missile crisis.

Another fear is that a presidential adviser in the White House will usurp the functions of the Secretary and the Department, leaving for them only formal and administrative duties. This bugaboo is constructed out of ignorance. No matter how ambitious an empire builder he may be, an adviser in the antechamber is restricted by limitations of time and staff to participation in formulation of policy—and few policies at that —to helping with speeches and messages expounding them, and to scrutinizing their execution. For the rest, both formulation and execution remain, and must remain, in the departments. What has been occurring has not been that the White House advisers have edged the foreign office out of functions being competently performed but that they have been needed to do what is not being done anywhere to the satisfaction of the man responsible, the President. Why, one may ask, is not the proper remedy to find a Secretary who will do or have done what is necessary? The answer unhappily is that such men are not easy to come by or bring in.

What has been happening over the years is the atrophy of the agencies in three departments especially charged with correlating intelligence of the most intricate variety with the planning of policy: in the State Department, the Policy Planning Staff; in the Defense Department, International Security Affairs; and comparable areas in the Central Intelligence Agency. It is widely remarked that even the excellent staff in the White House of two years ago, then the best in this field, has also been worn away through overwork and difficulty of replacement, leaving an unfilled gap. If it should disappear altogether, the State

# The Eclipse of the State Department

Department might lead a more relaxed existence, but the public interest would be less well served.

The foreign service officer by training and experience shies away from quantitative judgments and appraisals of economic and military power. Elsewhere I have quoted Professor Paul Y. Hammond: "at the extreme, the foreign service officer would . . . rely emphatically upon the personal skills and noncommunicable wisdom of the experienced career official and would view the requirements of large-scale organizations (such as the armed forces with their demands for forward planning) as a direct threat to the practice of this diplomatic art." To supplement the weakness of the career service General Marshall created the Policy Planning Staff. The subsequent loss of its original capacity weakened the Department. This is clear today in policies put forward for the Middle East, Africa, and the United Nations, almost all emerging from the Department. Knowledge of political developments and people in the areas concerned and the guidance of generalities, maxims, or convictions, usually moralistic in nature and strongly held at home, cannot substitute for a capacity in correlating forces when the need is for plotting courses through the complicated mine fields in these areas or in devising a strategy for nuclear negotiations with the Soviet Union. There is a place and work for many talents here.

The present eclipse of a position held by the State Department, though perhaps briefly, distresses me. I should have hated to have had to adjust myself to such a change. I far preferred the happier even though more turbulent circumstances under which I did serve. However, it is a mistake to believe that present arrangements are a disaster, or ill serve the public interest, or are due to presidential whimsy, or personal ambitions. If, however, whatever rare and valuable talents now available and used should be lost because "ignorant armies clash by night," the public will, indeed, have been ill served.